ARREST SEARCH AND SEIZURE IN GEORGIA

Edited by R. Ernest Taylor

CARL VINSON INSTITUTE OF GOVERNMENT
THE UNIVERSITY OF GEORGIA

ARREST/SEARCH AND SEIZURE IN GEORGIA

Editing: Inge Whittle (current edition); Ann Blum, Ruth Carpenter, Susan Jones (previous editions)
Proofreading: John Gaither
Typesetting: Anne Huddleston, Helen Kelley (current edition); Debra Peters (previous editions)
Design and production: Reid McCallister
Production: Mary Porter
Publications editor: Emily Honigberg

Appreciation is expressed to Captain Ernest M. Nix of the University of Georgia Police Department for providing the photographs from which the cover silhouettes were taken.

Copyright © 1985 by the Carl Vinson Institute of Government, The University of Georgia. Printed in the United States of America. All rights reserved. No part of this report may be used or reproduced in any manner whatsoever without written permission except in the case of brief quotations embodied in critical articles and reviews. For information, write Publications Program, Carl Vinson Institute of Government, Terrell Hall, University of Georgia, Athens, Georgia 30602.

Second Printing

Library of Congress Cataloging-in-Publication Data

Arrest/search and seizure in Georgia.
    Includes bibliographies and index.
    1. Arrest—Georgia. 2. Searches and seizures—Georgia
I. Taylor, R. Ernest
KF576.A97 1985   345.758'052   85-20166
ISBN 0-89854-111-5   347.580552

Foreword

The Carl Vinson Institute of Government first began developing and publishing manuals on arrest, search, and seizure in 1957. Since that time, there have been several revisions of two separate books: *Criminal Arrest in Georgia* and *Search and Seizure in Georgia*. These manuals have been used by law enforcement officers and by persons training new recruits. Since both subjects are generally taught or reviewed together, combining the two manuals into a single, comprehensive statement on the law of arrest, search, and seizure appeared to be a logical and cost effective approach.

This newly combined and revised publication, *Arrest/Search and Seizure in Georgia*, was developed to provide law enforcement officers in Georgia with a general reference to these two vital areas of law and to provide examples as guides to assist officers in their everyday routines. The manual is not intended as an exhaustive treatment of the law on arrest, search, and seizure and should not be relied on as such. The laws in these areas are constantly being shaped and reshaped by both the Georgia Supreme Court and the United States Supreme Court. Therefore the reader is urged to keep track of new decisions of these courts to see how they might affect the law as stated in this manual.

The editor of *Arrest/Search and Seizure* is R. Ernest Taylor of the Vinson Institute's Human Services Division, who also supervised the 1979 revision of the separate companion manuals. He was provided very able assistance by Donald Robert Black, Jr., and James Ellis Millsaps, both students of the University of Georgia School of Law. Many individuals have been involved in the production of *Arrest/Search and Seizure* over the years. We are grateful to Thomas H. Baxley, Rosa F. Beatty, Wm. John Camp, and John E. Settle, Jr., graduates of the University law school, for their research and to Hubert L. Grimes and Sharon Ward, formerly of the Institute, for their assistance in updating the manuals.

                    Melvin B. Hill, Jr.
                    Director
                    Carl Vinson Institute of Government

Contents

Part I: Arrest

I WHAT IS AN ARREST? _____ 3

    What constitutes arrest? / 3
        Stopping suspicious persons as constituting arrest / 3
        Stopping motor vehicles as constituting arrest / 4
    Endnotes / 4

II ARREST WITH A WARRANT _____ 6

    What is a warrant? / 6
        Contents of a warrant / 6
        Form of warrant / 8
        Identification of person to be arrested / 8
        Designation of offense charged / 9
    Who may issue warrants? / 9
    Necessity for probable cause / 10
    Informants' tips / 12
    The affidavit / 13
        Contents of an affidavit / 13
        Form of affidavit / 13
        Necessity for oath / 14
        Who may administer oath and receive affidavit? / 15
    Execution of warrant / 15
        Officer's duty to execute warrant / 15
        Who may not execute warrant? / 15
        Execution of warrant in county other than
            that in which issued / 16
        Execution of warrant in state other than
            that in which issued / 16
        Where are warrants returnable? / 17
    Endnotes / 17

III ARREST WITHOUT A WARRANT _____ 20

    When is warrantless arrest justified? / 20
        Arrest for offense committed
            in officer's presence / 20
        Arrest when offender is endeavoring to escape / 21

Arrest when there has been an act of
   family violence / 22
Arrest when there is likely to be
   a failure of justice / 22
Arrest to prevent felony / 23
Necessity for probable cause / 23
Promptness in making arrest without warrant / 23
Arrest of fugitives / 24
Rearrest / 24
Territorial extent of authority to arrest
   without warrant / 25
Endnotes / 27

IV ARREST BY PRIVATE CITIZENS — 30

Crimes justifying citizen's arrest / 30
   Citizen's arrest for misdemeanor / 30
   Citizen's arrest for felony / 30
   Citizen's arrest for violation of
     municipal ordinance / 31
Promptness in making citizen's arrest / 31
Additional authority / 32
   Authority of posse members / 32
   Authority of bondsmen / 32
   Authority of hospital staff regarding
     tuberculosis patients / 32
Duty upon making citizen's arrest / 32
Endnotes / 33

V PROCEDURE WHEN MAKING ARREST — 35

Possession of warrant at time of arrest / 35
Giving notice of authority / 36
Use of force / 36
Shooting or killing to prevent escape / 37
Entering private premises / 38
Stopping train / 38
Summoning assistance: posse / 38
When resistance is justified / 39
Endnotes / 39

VI RIGHTS AND DUTIES AFTER MAKING ARREST _____ 42

Duties to arrestees / 42
   Advising person arrested of constitutional rights / 42
   Care of property found in possession of
      person arrested / 42
Right to search incident to lawful arrest / 43
Commitment hearings / 43
   Right to commitment hearing / 43
   Who may hold commitment hearing? / 44
   Commitment hearing for person arrested
      under warrant / 44
   Commitment hearing for person arrested
      without warrant / 45
Accepting bail / 45
Keeping records / 46
Endnotes / 46

VII IMMUNITY FROM CRIMINAL ARREST _____ 48

Who enjoys immunity from criminal arrest? / 48
   Foreign representatives / 48
Limited immunity from criminal arrest / 48
   Members of Congress / 48
   Members of the General Assembly / 48
Immunity from arrest in civil cases / 49
   Who is exempt? / 49
Endnotes / 49

VIII LIABILITY AND JURISDICTION OF LAW ENFORCEMENT OFFICERS _____ 50

Officer liability / 50
Officer jurisdiction / 50
   Georgia State Patrol / 50
   Georgia Bureau of Investigation / 51
   City police / 51
   Sheriffs / 51
   County police / 51
   Marshals / 51
   Coroners / 51
   State revenue agents / 51

Prison guards, wardens, and correctional officers / 52
State conservation rangers / 52
State probation officers / 52
State drug inspectors / 52
State fire marshal / 53
Executive security guards / 53
Janitors and guards of public buildings / 53
Department of Human Resources institutional police / 53
Campus police / 53
Endnotes / 53

Part II: Search and Seizure — 55

IX SEARCH AND SEIZURE WITH A WARRANT — 57

What is a search warrant? / 57
   Contents of a search warrant / 60
   Particularity requirement of a search warrant / 60
Obtaining a search warrant / 61
   Who can get a warrant? / 61
   Who can issue a warrant? / 61
   How is a warrant obtained? / 62
Contents of an affidavit / 63
   Probable cause / 63
Executing a search warrant / 64
   Who may execute (carry out) a search warrant? / 64
   Time of execution / 64
   Entering the premises and the use of force / 65
   What may be seized? / 66
   Limitations on the search / 67
   Requirement to leave a copy of the warrant / 67
   Return to court of warrant, items seized, and inventory / 68
Endnotes / 68

X EXCEPTIONS TO THE SEARCH WARRANT REQUIREMENT — 71

Search and seizure by consent / 71
Plain view / 72
Search and seizure under exigent circumstances / 73
Search incident to a lawful arrest / 74
Endnotes / 76

XI SEARCH OF PREMISES WITHOUT A WARRANT _____ 78

Search of premises incident to a lawful arrest / 78
Hot pursuit / 79
Endnotes / 80

XII SEARCH OF THE PERSON WITHOUT A WARRANT _____ 81

Stop and frisk / 81
Search of person incident to a lawful arrest / 82
Search of the body / 83
Searches as part of police procedure / 84
Endnotes / 85

XIII SEARCHES AND SEIZURES INVOLVING VEHICLES _____ 87

Stopping and searching moving vehicles
    suspected of carrying contraband / 88
Search of the vehicle after it has been stopped / 89
Search of the vehicle following an arrest / 90
Searches pursuant to traffic violations,
    investigatory stops, and roadblocks / 91
Searches of abandoned vehicles / 93
Inventory searches of vehicles taken into
    police custody / 94
Search of vehicles with a warrant / 96
Endnotes / 98

XIV ELECTRONIC SURVEILLANCE AS SEARCH AND SEIZURE _____ 104

Conversations are protected / 104
Investigative warrant requirement / 105
    Execution of the warrant / 106
    Exceptions to the warrant requirement / 106
Endnotes / 107

XV EFFECTS OF AN ILLEGAL SEARCH AND SEIZURE — 108

Illegal searches with a warrant / 108
Illegal searches without a warrant / 109
Personal liability for illegal search and seizure / 109
    Consent — a defense to personal liability / 110
Endnotes / 111

FIGURES

Figure 1 — Form of warrant / 8
Figure 2 — Form of affidavit / 14
Figure 3 — Warning reminders / 43
Figure 4 — Affidavit and complaint for search warrant / 58-59

TABLE OF CASES / 113

TABLE OF STATUTES / 125

GLOSSARY / 129

INDEX / 133

PART 1
ARREST

What Is an Arrest?

WHAT CONSTITUTES ARREST?

An arrest is made whenever someone is taken, seized, or detained by any means which indicate an intention to take that person into custody and which subject him or her to the control and will of the person making the arrest.[1] It is not necessary that the person arrested actually be seized or even touched,[2] and no formal words of arrest need be spoken.[3] An arrest is simply whenever the liberty of a person to come and go as he or she pleases is restrained, no matter how slight.[4] It is sufficient if the person understands that he or she is under the control of the person making the arrest and submits to that control.[5] Even when the person arrested is allowed considerable freedom of movement, the arrest is complete—provided his or her movements are at the discretion of the person making the arrest.[6]

Stopping Suspicious Persons as Constituting Arrest

When an individual is accosted by a law enforcement officer and subjected to questioning, an arrest has been made if the officer restrains the individual's freedom to walk away. This is the case regardless of whether the officer intends to make a **technical arrest**, that is, one resulting in the prosecution of a crime.

It is possible, however, to conduct an **investigative detention** under circumstances not amounting to an arrest. An officer may stop a suspect if he or she has **reasonable suspicion** that criminal activity might be afoot.[7] (Reasonable suspicion is that based on the officer's natural senses, experience, and good judgment.) After identifying him- or herself, the officer may question the suspect as to name, address, reason for presence, etc. However, the failure of the person to answer the questions does not alone justify an arrest.

In addition to questioning, the officer may, on the basis of a reasonable suspicion that the suspect is armed and dangerous, frisk the person.[8] A frisk, which is actually a search, is limited to a pat down of the suspect's outer clothing or garments for a gun or other weapon.[9] The sole justification for a frisk in such circumstances is the protection of the police officer: its scope is limited accordingly. The officer may make a warrantless arrest if a concealed weapon is discovered.[10]

It is important for the police officer to remember that a **stop and frisk** is actually a two-step process—a reasonable suspicion is necessary for the stop and for the frisk.[11] Thus, a frisk producing drugs would be illegal if the person stopped were not suspected of being armed and dangerous.[12] Officers would be justified, however, in frisking a suspect who met a fugitive's description if, while questioning the suspect, they saw a suspicious bulge under his or her clothes.[13]

Stopping Motor Vehicles as Constituting Arrest

Since driving a motor vehicle on the streets and highways of this state is considered a privilege rather than a constitutional right, no arrest takes place when a motor vehicle is stopped for reasonable questioning of the occupants. This is true, for example, when an officer stops a vehicle to make an appropriate driver's license check.[14] It also holds when, with reasonable cause, an officer stops a vehicle to determine whether it complies with Georgia safety standards.[15] However, if the vehicle is stopped to place some non-traffic-related criminal charge, then an arrest has taken place from the moment the officer approaches the vehicle and causes the suspect to alight from it under force and restraint, and all the formalities of an arrest attach.[16]

ENDNOTES

1. Conoly v. Imperial Tobacco Co., 63 Ga. App. 880, 885, 12 S.E. 2d 398, 403 (1940).
2. OFFICIAL CODE OF GA. ANN. (O.C.G.A.) §17-4-1; Hines v. Adams, 27 Ga. App. 157, 158, 107 S.E. 618, 619 (1921).
3. *See* Barron v. State, 109 Ga. App. 786, 787-88, 137 S.E. 2d 690, 693 (1964); United States v. Jones, 352 F. Supp. 369 (S.D. Ga. 1972).

4. Tolbert v. Hicks, 158 Ga. App. 642, 281 S.E. 2d 368 (1981).
5. O.C.G.A. §17-4-1; Conoly v. Imperial Tobacco Co., 63 Ga. App. 880, 885, 12 S.E. 2d 398, 403 (1940).
6. O.C.G.A. §17-4-1; Courtoy v. Dozier, 20 Ga. 369 (1856).
7. Terry v. Ohio, 392 U.S. 1 (1968); Barnwell v. State, 127 Ga. App. 335, 193 S.E. 2d 203 (1972).
8. *Id.*
9. O.C.G.A. §17-5-1.
10. Holtzendorf v. State, 125 Ga. App. 747, 188 S.E. 2d 879 (1972).
11. Jones v. State, 126 Ga. App. 841, 192 S.E. 2d 171 (1972).
12. Bethea v. State, 127 Ga. App. 97, 192 S.E. 2d 554 (1972); *see* Sibron v. New York, 392 U.S. 41, 62 (1968).
13. Alexander v. State, 225 Ga. 358, 168 S.E. 2d 315 (1969).
14. *See* O.C.G.A. §40-5-57.
15. O.C.G.A. §40-8-200.
16. Clement v. State, 226 Ga. 66, 172 S.E. 2d 600 (1970).

Arrest with a Warrant

WHAT IS A WARRANT?

The liberty of the individual citizen is guarded jealously by the law.[1] The rule, therefore, is that, except for a limited number of exceptional cases, no lawful arrest may be made without a valid arrest warrant.[2] (Chapter 3 discusses arrest without a warrant.) The law would prefer that all arrests be made with a warrant, since the warrant requirement interjects an impartial magistrate or other judicial officer between the arresting officer and the arrestee to determine whether sufficient evidence exists for an arrest to be made. An **arrest warrant** is a judicial command to arrest a particular individual and to bring the arrestee promptly before the magistrate issuing the warrant or some other judicial officer. *There is no such thing as an oral or a telephone warrant.*[3]

A valid warrant must be based on the personal knowledge of the issuing magistrate or on an accusation by someone else sworn to in an affidavit.[4] Both the warrant and the affidavit must comply fully with certain statutory requirements. (See "Contents of a Warrant," below, and "Contents of an Affidavit," p. 13.)

A warrant may be issued in any county in Georgia, even for a crime committed in another county. Once issued, a warrant may be carried from one county to another, and it may be served in any county of the state regardless of where it was issued.[5]

Contents of a Warrant

A valid arrest warrant must contain specific information required by statute or made necessary by court decisions.

An early Georgia case requires that the following information be given in the warrant:[6]

1. The authority under which the warrant is issued must be indicated.
2. The person who is to execute the warrant must be identified. (Generally, this is accomplished by addressing the warrant "to any sheriff, deputy sheriff, coroner, constable, marshal, or police officer.")
3. The person(s) to be arrested must be identified.

The Official Code of Georgia Annotated (O.C.G.A.) requires that warrants contain the following additional information:[7]

4. The offense committed must be designated.
5. The time, date, and place of occurrence of the offense must be given, including the county in which it was committed.
6. The person against whom the offense was committed must be identified.
7. The offense must be fully described. (See "Designation of Offense Charged," p. 9.)

When the offense charged is larceny, the Georgia Code* requires that the warrant be more detailed. It must, in addition, include the following information:[8]

8. The property alleged to have been stolen must be identified and described.
9. The owner must be named.
10. The value of the property must be given.
11. The person from whose possession it was taken must be named.

The purpose of the statutory requirements is to inform the person arrested of the specific charges against him or her.[9] Minimal compliance with these requirements is not enough: unless they are met strictly, the warrant will not be valid.[10]

---

*Note that the word(s) "Code" or "Georgia Code" will be used throughout the text rather than the longer "Official Code of Georgia Annotated."

Form of Warrant

The Georgia Code gives a form for warrants, as shown in Figure 1, and provides that compliance with it shall be sufficient in all cases.[11]

Identification of Person to Be Arrested

For a warrant to be valid, it is absolutely essential that the person sought for arrest can be identified from the contents of the warrant. The usual method of identifying someone is by inserting the person's name in the warrant, but a warrant may be valid even though the name of the accused does not appear. If the warrant does not contain a name, it must contain other information sufficient to make identification possible. This may be done by stating the occupation of the accused, his or her personal appearance, peculiarities, and/or place of residence, or by giving some other means of identification.[12]

Figure 1. *Form of Warrant*

Georgia, _____ County.
To any sheriff, deputy sheriff, coroner, constable, or marshal of said State—Greeting:
    A. B. makes oath before me that on the ____ day of _____, in the year 19____, in the county aforesaid, C. D. did commit the offense of *(insert here all information describing offense as required by Code section 17-4-41).* You are therefore commanded to arrest the body of said C. D., and bring him before me, or some other judicial officer of this State, to be dealt with as the law directs. You will also levy on a sufficiency of the property of said C. D. to pay the costs in the event of his final conviction. Herein fail not.

_____, Judicial Officer

Peace officers commonly misunderstand the legality of so-called **John Doe warrants**. A warrant issued for John Doe is valid only if it contains a description sufficient for identification[13] by an officer who has no personal knowledge of the suspect. In contrast, a blank warrant for an unknown suspect (John Doe), later completed, is fatally defective.

Designation of Offense Charged

In accordance with statutory requirements,[14] a warrant must name and describe fully the offense with which the person sought is charged. Thus, a warrant which merely alleged "the crime of misdemeanor" would be invalid because it failed to describe how the offense was committed, or even to name it.[15]

In describing the commission of the offense, a warrant must allege every constituent element of the crime charged.[16] In Georgia, there are no crimes except those set forth by statute.[17] For example, issuing a check without sufficient funds is a crime if certain conditions, including an intent to defraud, are present.[18] Accordingly, a warrant charging someone only with "passing a worthless check" would be invalid unless it also alleged that the check was passed "with intent to defraud."[19]

WHO MAY ISSUE WARRANTS?

The Georgia Code authorizes the following officials to issue warrants for the arrest of offenders against the penal laws of Georgia:[20]

- superior court judges
- magistrates
- municipal officials legally given the powers of a magistrate

These officials may issue warrants on the basis of their personal knowledge or, as is more often the case, on the information of others given to them under oath in an affidavit.[21] (See "Contents of an Affidavit" and "Form of Affidavit," pp. 13 and 14.)

These affidavits are usually filed by peace officers in the performance of their official duties. However, the procurement of warrants of arrest is not their exclusive prerogative or privilege: any private citizen may procure the issuance of a warrant by following the same procedure.[22]

10 / ARREST

In counties where there is no city or county court, the county probate judge possesses warrant-issuing power in misdemeanor cases arising under the Georgia State Highway Patrol Act of 1937, other traffic laws, and the compulsory school attendance law.[23]

In addition, a county coroner may issue a warrant of arrest, returnable as other warrants, if an inquest discloses facts that may lead to the prosecution of a suspect for homicide.[24]

Municipal officials sometimes have warrant-issuing authority even though they are not, by statute, specifically granted the powers of a magistrate. For example, a municipal charter may give the mayor the duty of seeing that town ordinances are obeyed and the jurisdiction to try persons charged with violating such ordinances. The mayor then has the authority to issue arrest warrants for violators. This is true even if the charter does not, in express terms, authorize the mayor to issue warrants.[25]

Since issuing an arrest warrant is a judicial act, it normally may not be performed by nonjudicial officials such as court clerks.[26] However, exceptions have been made by the General Assembly.[27] Thus, where a statute created a municipal court and provided that clerks and deputy clerks could take affidavits and issue warrants, it was held within the power of these officials to do so.[28]

In some situations, other officials of state government exercise warrant-issuing authority. Members of the State Board of Pardons and Paroles, for example, may issue warrants for parolees or conditional releasees who have violated the terms of their releases.[29] In addition, the governor may issue warrants for the arrest of fugitives from other states.[30]

Warrants for the arrest of a peace officer for offenses allegedly committed while performing his or her duties may be issued only by a judge of a superior court, state court, or probate court.[31]

NECESSITY FOR PROBABLE CAUSE

Before issuing an arrest warrant, a magistrate must receive an affidavit under oath or have personal knowledge showing **probable cause** that the person sought has committed an offense.[32] This procedure assures that the question of probable cause is determined by a disinterested and impartial magistrate rather than by a police officer or other person directly interested in seeing that an arrest is made.[33]

Probable cause has been defined as

> [a] reasonable ground of suspicion, supported by circumstances sufficiently strong in themselves to warrant a cautious man in the belief that the party is guilty of the offense with which he is charged.[34]

If this reasonable ground of suspicion is present, an arrest warrant can be issued. Probable cause may be based on evidence that would not justify condemnation or even be admissible in a criminal trial.[35] For example, an affidavit containing hearsay evidence may provide probable cause and form the basis for a warrant, if there are substantial grounds for believing the hearsay.[36]

An arrest warrant may be issued upon an indictment, of course, since the grand jury's determination that probable cause exists for the indictment establishes that element for the purpose of the warrant.[37] An arrest warrant based on a statutorily complete affidavit (see p. 13) is deemed to have impliedly met the requirement of probable cause, and the arrest warrant is properly issued.[38]

It is important for peace officers to realize that probable cause for arrest does not necessarily constitute probable cause for a search warrant. (See *Part II, Search and Seizure,* "Search and Seizure with a Warrant," p. 57.) Conversely, probable cause for a search warrant necessarily provides grounds for arrest. Each requires the same amount of evidence, but relating to somewhat different facts and circumstances.

For an arrest, two conclusions that must be supported by evidence are that

1. an offense has been committed and
2. the person to be arrested committed it.

By comparison, for search there must be probable cause that

1. the items sought are connected with criminal activity and
2. the items will be found in the place to be searched.

A party arrested without probable cause has a right to recourse if the arrest is made maliciously.[39] Thus, the accuser may be liable to the party arrested if the circumstances indicate to a jury that he or she had no grounds for the proceeding but a desire to injure the accused.[40]

INFORMANTS' TIPS

An officer may make an arrest, with or without a warrant, based on information received from an informant. It must be shown, however, that the tip was reliable and, thus, that probable cause for the arrest existed before it was effected.[41] If a police officer acts upon the word of an informant of unproved reliability, probable cause may exist if other circumstantial evidence tends to establish guilt.[42]

When the arrest is made solely on the basis of the informant's information, the affidavit must meet two conditions—informant credibility and basis for the conclusion reached by the informant. A discussion of each follows.

1. The affidavit must reveal underlying circumstances showing reason to believe that the informant is a credible person.[43]

The following factors are often considered in determining the credibility of an informant:

    a. length of time the officer has known or dealt with the informant
    b. general character and reputation of the informant
    c. number of tips received from the informant in the past
    d. accuracy of the information previously given
    e. whether the informant has volunteered or been paid for information

2. The affidavit must reveal underlying circumstances showing the basis of the conclusion reached by the informant.[44]

This requirement of an affidavit can be satisfied by a statement of the informant's personal observations[45] or assumptions, and the reasons therefor.[46] In contrast, a disclosure that the informant received the information from a third party would be inadequate unless it was determined that the ultimate source of the information was also credible and reliably informed on the matter.

Both requirements use the words "underlying circumstances." In Georgia, "circumstances" have recently been interpreted to mean that the affidavit must contain sufficient facts to show: (a) support for the informant's reliability; (b) that the affidavit specifically states how the informant obtained his or her information and describes the alleged criminal act in such detail that the magistrate may know that it is more than casual rumor circulating in the underworld or is an accusation based only on an individual's general reputation; and (c) that the information is not stale.[47] The phrase "the information is not stale" has been defined by the courts as "a time period closely related to the commission of the offense [which] must be affirmatively stated within the affidavit."[48]

If the underlying circumstances concerning the informant's credibility, the source of his or her information, or even both are not disclosed, the informant's tip may, nonetheless, be considered in determining whether there is probable cause. Although the tip then clearly needs additional support, the amount of corroborating information needed depends on the circumstances of the case. When the source of the informant's information is not disclosed, the informant must have given enough details, when they are corroborated, to justify the conclusion that his or her source was reliable.[49]

THE AFFIDAVIT

Contents of an Affidavit

An affidavit, like a warrant, must meet certain statutory requirements as to content. The Code requires that to be valid, an affidavit must contain the same information required of a warrant.[50] (See Contents of a Warrant, p. 6.) When the offense charged is larceny, the affidavit must contain the same additional details.[51] As in the case of a warrant, mere substantial compliance with the statutory requirements is not sufficient and will invalidate an affidavit.[52]

While compliance with the statutory requirements is essential, it is not likely that an affidavit would be invalidated by a mere verbal inaccuracy, where the meaning is nonetheless clear, or by a minor technical error. Thus, it is not a fatal defect to follow the names of the accused with a singular pronoun, such as "her" or "him," where the sense calls for a plural pronoun, such as "their" or "them."[53] Further, an affidavit will not be invalidated if the person who makes the affidavit signs it at a spot other than on the line provided for his or her signature.[54] Errors such as these do not make it appear any less likely that probable cause for an arrest exists.

Form of Affidavit

The Code gives a form for an affidavit (see Figure 2) and provides that compliance with it shall be sufficient in all cases.[55]

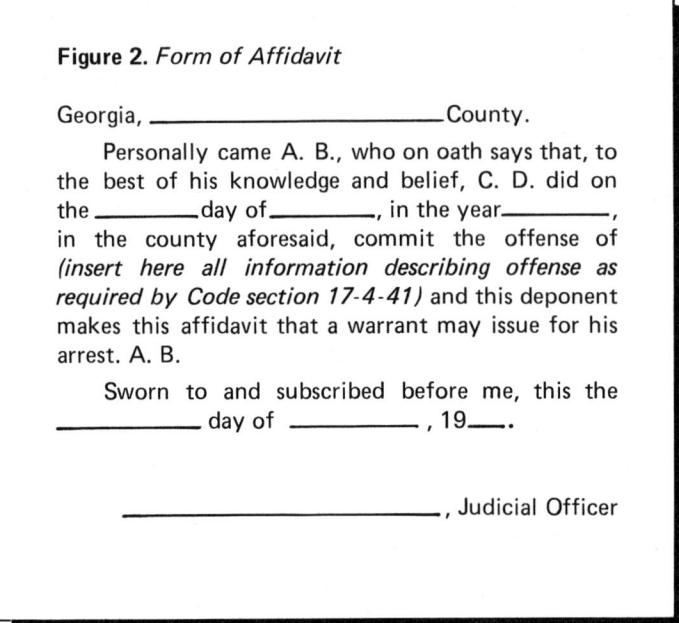

Figure 2. *Form of Affidavit*

Georgia, _____ County.

 Personally came A. B., who on oath says that, to the best of his knowledge and belief, C. D. did on the _____ day of _____, in the year_____, in the county aforesaid, commit the offense of *(insert here all information describing offense as required by Code section 17-4-41)* and this deponent makes this affidavit that a warrant may issue for his arrest. A. B.

 Sworn to and subscribed before me, this the _____ day of _____ , 19___.

_____ , Judicial Officer

Necessity for Oath

No judge has authority to issue an arrest warrant on the basis of another person's claims that a crime has been committed unless those claims are sworn to under oath.[56] Therefore, before an affidavit can become the basis for an arrest warrant and for any further legal proceeding it must meet some requirements. It must appear that an oath was actually administered to the person making the affidavit, or that person must do something to signify that he or she has consciously accepted the obligation of an oath.[57]

The law has not prescribed any exact words or special ceremony that must be used to validate the administration of an oath.[58] It is not necessary that the oath be formal or that the person making the affidavit hold up a hand and swear. It is necessary only that some action be taken in the presence of the official receiving the affidavit whereby both the affiant and the official understand that what is done is all that is necessary to complete the act of swearing.[59]

Contrary to the rule in some states,[60] the facts in an affidavit need be sworn to as true but only that they are true to the best of the affiant's knowledge and belief.[61]

Who May Administer Oath and Receive Affidavit?

To form the basis of an arrest warrant, an affidavit must be sworn to before an official authorized by law to administer oaths and take affidavits. Such officials include all those who are authorized to issue warrants (see p. 7).[62]

Since taking an affidavit in a criminal proceeding imposes a duty of a judicial nature, an affidavit sworn to before a nonjudicial officer such as a court clerk, without the presence of the judge of the court, usually is not sufficient basis for an arrest warrant.[63] However, the power to take affidavits has been granted at times to clerks and other nonjudicial officers by the General Assembly.[64] When this has been done, a warrant may be based on an affidavit sworn to before a clerk.[65]

EXECUTION OF WARRANT

Officer's Duty to Execute Warrant

When a warrant, valid in form and issued by a court of competent jurisdiction, is placed in the hands of a law enforcement officer for execution, the officer has no choice but to serve it. "Every officer," according to the Georgia Code, "is bound to execute the penal warrants placed in his hands."[66] Refusal to do so constitutes an offense for which the officer may be indicted.[67]

An officer serving a warrant must be sure that the person arrested is the person identified by the warrant and no one else.[68] If the person is identified by name, the arresting officer must see that the person arrested bears the name specified in the warrant. The arrest will be legal if he or she bears that name, even if it later appears that the person arrested was not the person intended.[69]

If there are two or more persons in the officer's jurisdiction with the same name, however, the officer must attempt to ascertain, before making an arrest, for which person the warrant was intended. If the officer decides this question in good faith, the arrest is lawful—even though the officer may make a mistake and arrest the wrong person.[70] If the person to be arrested is identified only by description, the officer must see that the person arrested fits the description in the warrant. Again, if this question is decided in good faith, the arrest is legal.[71]

Who May Not Execute Warrant?

The Supreme Court of Georgia has termed it improper for the person who made the affidavit upon which the warrant was based to make the arrest.[72] This is clearly true where the person making the affidavit is a private citizen who has been deputized,[73] even if his or her name does not appear on the warrant.[74] Whether the situation would be the same in the case of a regular police officer is uncertain, since this point has not been specifically determined in a court decision.[75] Certainly, an officer may swear out a warrant and have another officer make the arrest.[76] And there seems to be no policy against an officer who swears out a warrant going with other officers to execute it.[77]

Execution of Warrant in County Other Than That in Which Issued

The general rule in the United States is that, in the absence of statutory authority, an arrest may not be made either outside the territorial jurisdiction of the magistrate issuing a warrant or outside the territorial jurisdiction of the officer to whom the warrant is addressed.[78] In Georgia, however, as in some other states, the general rule has been modified by statute. The Code provides that an arresting officer may execute a warrant in any county of the state without regard to the residence of the officer.[79] Thus, a sheriff is not limited to the geographical boundaries of his or her own county and may travel to a distant part of the state to execute a warrant.

The authority to cross county lines to execute warrants is granted, however, only to officers who derive their arrest powers from the state law. It does not extend to city police officers whose authority to arrest is found in municipal ordinances. Thus, a city police officer has no legal authority to go beyond the geographical limits of the municipality of which he or she is an officer to serve a warrant.[80] It has been held, however, that a state officer may call city police officers as a posse and may deputize them to help serve a warrant beyond the limits of their city.[81]

Execution of Warrant in State Other Than That in Which Issued

An arrest warrant issued in one state may not be executed in another, because it has no validity beyond the boundaries of the state by whose authority it was issued.[82] Even so, it may provide reasonable information in another state so as to justify the arrest of a fugitive without a warrant under the Uniform Criminal Extradition Act.[83]

Where Are Warrants Returnable?

With the exception of judges of superior courts, no judicial officers may issue a warrant for arrest returnable only before him- or herself.[84] Thus, a warrant issued by any other judicial officer is a general arrest warrant and must be made returnable before that officer or before "any other judicial officer having jurisdiction."[85] However, the judicial officer before whom the prisoner is brought must be an officer of the county in which the offense is alleged to have been committed.[86]

A superior court judge may issue a "special warrant" returnable only before him- or herself, but only within the judge's own judicial circuits.[87] If any superior court judge issues a special warrant outside his or her judicial circuit, the warrant shall be treated as a general arrest warrant.[88]

ENDNOTES

1. Porter v. State, 124 Ga. 297, 302, 52 S.E. 283, 285 (1905).
2. Thomas v. State, 91 Ga. 204, 206, 18 S.E. 305 (1892); Smith v. State, 84 Ga. App. 79, 82, 65 S.E. 2d 709, 711 (1951).
3. Walker v. State, 220 Ga. 415, 419-20, 139 S.E. 2d 278, 282 (1964), rev'd on other grounds 381 U.S. 355 (1965).
4. OFFICIAL CODE OF GA. ANN. (O.C.G.A.) §17-4-70.
5. O.C.G.A. §17-4-44.
6. Brady v. Davis, 9 Ga. 73, 75 (1850).
7. O.C.G.A. § 17-4-41.
8. *Id*. Since the Code of Criminal Procedure was written in 1972, the distinctions between larceny and theft are preserved in regards to the issuing of arrest warrants.
9. *Id.*
10. Lowe v. Turner, 115 Ga. App. 503, 505, 154 S.E. 2d 792, 794 (1967); Lovett v. State, 111 Ga. App. 295, 141 S.E. 2d 595 (1965).
11. O.C.G.A. §17-4-46.
12. Blocker v. Clark, 126 Ga. 484, 486-87, 54 S.E. 1022, 1023 (1906); Fomby v. State, 120 Ga. App. 387, 170 S.E. 2d 585 (1969).
13. *Id.*
14. For a list of the statutory requirements, *see* "Contents of Warrant," p. 6.
15. Lovett v. State, 111 Ga. App. 295, 141 S.E. 2d 595 (1965).
16. Lowe v. Turner, 115 Ga. App. 593, 154 S.E. 2d 792 (1967).
17. Savannah News-Press, Inc. v. Harley, 100 Ga. App. 387, 111 S.E. 2d 259 (1959).
18. O.C.G.A. §16-9-20.
19. Lowe v. Turner, 115 Ga. App. 593, 505, 154 S.E. 2d 792, 795 (1967).
20. O.C.G.A. §17-4-40.
21. *Id.*

22. Cleland v. United States Fidelity and Guar. Ins. Co., 99 Ga. App. 130, 107 S.E. 2d 904 (1959).
23. Ga. Const. art. VI. sec. IX, par. II (1982).
24. O.C.G.A. §45-16-35.
25. Williams v. Sewell, 121 Ga. 665, 49 S.E. 732 (1905).
26. Cox v. Perkins, 151 Ga. 632, 107 S.E. 863 (1921).
27. Ormond v. Ball, 120 Ga. 916, 921, 48 S.E. 383, 385 (1904).
28. Wadley v. McCommon, 154 Ga. 420, 114 S.E. 357 (1922).
29. O.C.G.A. §42-9-48.
30. O.C.G.A. §§17-13-20 through 17-13-30.
31. O.C.G.A. §17-4-40.
32. U.S. Const. Amend. IV; Ga. Const. art. I, sec. I, par. III (1982).
33. Giordenello v. United States, 357 U.S. 480, 486 (1958).
34. Stacey v. Emery, 97 U.S. 642, 645 (1878).
35. United States v. Ventresca, 380 U.S. 102, 107 (1965); Johnson v. State, 111 Ga. App. 298, 304, 141 S.E. 2d 574, 580 (1965).
36. United States v. Ventresca, 380 U.S. 102, 108 (1965).
37. Giordenello v. United States, 357 U.S. 480 (1958).
38. Davis v. State, 155 Ga. App. 511, 271 S.E. 2d 648 (1980).
39. O.C.G.A. §51-7-1.
40. O.C.G.A. §51-7-3.
41. Draper v. United States, 358 U.S. 307 (1958); Johnson v. State, 111 Ga. App. 298, 141 S.E. 2d 574 (1965).
42. Newcomb v. United States, 327 F.2d 649 (1964).
43. Aguilar v. Texas, 378 U.S. 108 (1964); U.S. v. Ventresca, 380 U.S. 102 (1969); Buck v. State, 127 Ga. App. 72, 192 S.E. 2d 432 (1972).
44. *Id.*
45. *Id.* Burns v. State, 119 Ga. App. 678; 168 S.E. 2d 786 (1969).
46. U.S. v. Ventresca, 380 U.S. 102 (1965); Campbell v. State, 226 Ga. 883, 178 S.E. 2d 257 (1970).
47. Daily v. State, 136 Ga. App. 866 222 S.E. 2d 682 (1975).
48. Bell v. State, 128 Ga. App. 426, 427, 196 S.E. 2d 894, 895 (1973).
49. *See* Draper v. United States, 358 U.S. 307 (1958); Spinelli v. United States, 393 U.S. 410 (1969); Johnston v. State, 227 Ga. 387, 181 S.E. 2d 42 (1971).
50. O.C.G.A. §17-4-41.
51. O.C.G.A. §17-4-41.5 For the additional details required of a warrant in larceny cases, *see* "Contents of a Warrant," p. 4, and *supra* at note 8.
52. Lowe v. Turner, 115 Ga. App. 503, 505, 154 S.E. 2d 792, 794 (1967); Lovett v. State, 111 Ga. App. 295, 141 S.E. 2d 595 (1965).
53. Dickson v. State, 62 Ga. 583 (1879).
54. Hardin v. State, 203 Ga. 641, 645, 47 S.E. 2d 745, 747 (1948).
55. O.C.G.A. §17-4-45.
56. O.C.G.A. §17-4-40.
57. Segars v. Cornwell, 128 Ga. App. 245, 196 S.E. 2d 341 (1973).
58. Britt v. Davis, 130 Ga. 74, 77, 60 S.E. 180, 181 (1908).

59. McCain v. Bonner 122 Ga. 842, 846, 51 S.E. 36, 38 (1905).
60. 5 Am. Jur. 2d *Arrest* §14 (1962).
61. O.C.G.A. §17-4-45.
62. O.C.G.A. § 17-4-40.
63. Cox v. Perkins, 151 Ga. 632, 107 S.E. 863 (1921).
64. Ormond v. Ball, 120 Ga. 916, 921, 48 S.E. 383, 385 (1904).
65. Green v. State, 49 Ga. App. 252, 255, 175 S.E. 26, 28 (1934).
66. O.C.G.A. §17-4-24.
67. Ormond v. Ball, 120 Ga. 916, 923-25, 48 S.E. 383, 386-87 (1904); Newkirk v. State, 57 Ga. App. 803, 807, 196 S.E. 911, 913 (1938).
68. Massey Stores, Inc. v. Reeves, 111 Ga. App. 227, 229, 141 S.E. 2d 227, 228 (1965).
69. Blocker v. Clark, 126 Ga. 484, 488-89, 54 S.E. 1022, 1023-24 (1906).
70. *Id.*
71. *Id.*
72. Cooper v. Lunsford, 203 Ga. 166, 174, 45 S.E. 2d 395, 400 (1947); McCray v. State, 134 Ga. 416, 426-27, 68 S.E. 62, 67 (1910); Davis v. State, 79 Ga. 767, 4 S.E. 318 (1887).
73. McCray v. State, 134 Ga. 416, 68 S.E. 62 (1910).
74. *Id.*
75. Cooper v. Lunsford, 203 Ga. 166, 174, 45 S.E. 2d 395, 400 (1947); Davis v. State, 79 Ga. 767, 4 S.E. 318 (1887).
76. *See* Cleland v. United States Fidelity and Guar. Ins. Co., 99 Ga. App. 130, 107 S.E. 2d 904 (1959).
77. Dye v. State, 114 Ga. App. 299, 151 S.E. 2d 164 (1966).
78. 5 Am.Jur. 2d *Arrest* §18 (1962); 6 C.J.S. *Arrest* §12 (1937); Annot., 61 A.L.R. 377 (1929).
79. O.C.G.A. §§17-4-44, 17-4-25.
80. Blair v. State, 90 Ga. 326, 17 S.E. 96 (1892); Coker v. State, 14 Ga. App. 606, 81 S.E. 818 (1914).
81. Phillips v. State, 66 Ga. 755 (1881).
82. 5 Am.Jur. 2d *Arrest* §20 (1962); 6 C.J.S. *Arrest* §12 (1937); Annot., 61 A.L.R. 377 (1929).
83. O.C.G.A. §17-13-34.
84. O.C.G.A. §17-4-42.
85. Ormond v. Ball, 120 Ga. 916, 921, 48 S.E. 383, 385 (1904).
86. O.C.G.A. §17-4-25.
87. O.C.G.A. §17-4-42.
88. *Id.*

Arrest without a Warrant

WHEN IS WARRANTLESS ARREST JUSTIFIED?

Ordinarily, an arrest should not be made without a warrant, and, except in certain exceptional situations, an arrest without a warrant is unlawful.[1] The Georgia Code specifies four situations in which an officer may legally make an arrest without a warrant:[2]

1. when an offense is committed in the officer's presence
2. when an offender is endeavoring to escape
3. when an officer has probable cause to believe that an act of family violence has been committed[3]
4. when for other cause there is likely to be failure of justice for want of a judicial officer to issue a warrant

An arrest without a warrant may be made when justified regardless of whether the offense is a misdemeanor or a felony.[4] However, somewhat greater latitude may be allowed in felony cases.[5]

The right to arrest without a warrant applies equally to municipal officers, such as policemen and town marshals, and to officers, such as sheriffs and constables, who derive their authority from state laws. Such arrests may be made for violations of municipal ordinances as well as state laws.[6]

Arrest for Offense Committed in Officer's Presence

An officer can arrest without a warrant for an offense committed in his or her presence even when that officer does not see the crime committed.[7] **Within the officer's immediate**

knowledge is the equivalent of **in the officer's presence**. Thus, a crime is committed in an officer's presence, or within his or her immediate knowledge, if, by seeing, hearing, or using any other senses, the officer has personal knowledge of its commission.[8] For example, an officer is justified in arresting a person without a warrant if the officer hears a shot and finds the suspect running from the place where the shot was fired,[9] or if the officer hears the noise of a beating and the cries of the person assaulted coming from within a house.[10] However, the mere smell of whiskey is insufficient, by itself, to authorize a warrantless arrest for illegal possession of liquor.[11]

An offense is not committed within an officer's immediate knowledge when it is reported to him or her by someone else.[12] Thus, an officer has no authority to arrest without a warrant merely upon information that someone is carrying a concealed pistol.[13] However, such an arrest is justified if the officer actually discerns the concealed weapon, for example, by seeing a bulge in a suspect's pocket.[14]

Georgia law specifically provides for the warrantless arrest of persons accused of violating any law or ordinance governing the operation, licensing, registration, maintenance, and inspection of motor vehicles, by the issuance of a citation, provided such offense is committed in the presence of the law enforcement officer.[15]

However, a law enforcement officer may effect a warrantless arrest upon receiving information from a law enforcement officer who observed the offense being committed, provided such information would constitute the basis for arrest had it been committed in the arresting officer's presence.[16] The citation issued must list the names of each officer, and both must be present when charges against the offender are heard. In instances where a motor vehicle offense results in an accident, the investigating officer may issue citations regardless of whether the offense occurred in the presence of a law enforcement officer.[17]

Arrest When Offender Is Endeavoring to Escape

An officer may arrest without a warrant when a suspect attempts to escape or flee, but unless there is an actual attempt to flee, the arrest will not be justified.[18] Thus, an officer may arrest without a warrant a suspect running from the scene of a shooting[19] or leaving the neighborhood of a crime by train.[20] Police also are justified in pursuing and arresting someone who refuses to stop his or her automobile when signaled to do so.[21]

However, when an officer discovers the suspect quietly seated and making no effort to flee, the officer may not justify an arrest without a warrant on the grounds that the suspect was attempting to escape.[22]

Arrest When There Has Been an Act of Family Violence

Officers must rely on good judgment when responding to family violence situation. Family violence means the occurrence of any felony and/or the commission of the offenses of assault, battery, criminal damage to property, unlawful restraint, and/or criminal trespass between spouses, parent and child(ren) or other persons related by consanguinity or affinity, and living in the same household. This definition does *not* include reasonable[23] discipline administered by a parent to a child in the form of corporal punishment, restraint, or detention.[24] These provisions were added to the Code in 1981 and have not yet been interpreted by the courts. Therefore, it is not known whether or not an arrest without a warrant can always be made immediately, even if there is an opportunity to obtain a warrant, or whether this section of the Code is merely a specific elaboration of situation 1 (offense in officer's presence) and/or 4 (likely to be a failure of justice) as listed on page 20. It would be prudent of an officer who is acting in response to a family violence situation, to obtain a warrant if an opportunity to do so exists.

Arrest When There Is Likely to Be a Failure of Justice

The meaning of the expression **likely to be a failure of justice for want of a judicial officer to issue a warrant** is somewhat obscure.[25] It is clear, however, that to justify a warrantless arrest under this statutory exception, there must be something more than the mere possibility of a failure of justice. An officer must have probable grounds for believing that there *will be a failure of justice* unless he or she makes an arrest without a warrant.[26] For example, officers acting on a storekeeper's complaint were justified in arresting a man without a warrant as he left the store where he had passed a bad check. Although the offense was not committed in the presence of the officers, the Georgia Court of Appeals held that there probably would have been a failure of justice for lack of a magistrate to issue a warrant if the arrest had not been made immediately.[27] In a similar case, the Georgia Supreme Court held that an arrest was not justified on the basis of a likely failure of justice where the facts revealed that the sheriff was in the county seat, and no mention was made of the unavailability of an officer to issue a warrant.28 Generally, the burden is on the police officer to show that no judicial officer was available to issue a warrant.29

Arrest to Prevent Felony

Although not listed among the statutory exceptions, there is a fifth situation in which an arrest without a warrant may be permissible. Officers apparently are justified in making a warrantless arrest to prevent the commission of a felony.30 Thus, the arrest without a warrant of a woman who told officers she intended to commit murder was permissible to prevent her from doing so.31 However, warrantless arrests to prevent felonies that have not yet been attempted probably are justified only when the criminal act is imminent.32

NECESSITY FOR PROBABLE CAUSE

When an officer arrests without a warrant, neither good faith by itself33 nor an unfounded suspicion that the person arrested may have committed a crime34 is enough to justify this action. The officer must have "reasonable grounds to suspect" that the person he or she arrests has committed an offense.35 The phrase **reasonable grounds to suspect** is the equivalent of the more common expression **probable cause**.36

What constitutes reasonable grounds of suspicion, or probable cause, is generally to be determined under the facts of each case. But, as a rule of thumb, the grounds of suspicion should be at least the same as would be required to obtain an arrest warrant.37 That is to say that probable cause is determined at the instant of the arrest, not by evidence acquired after the arrest. Thus, officers are not justified in arresting a suspicious person without a warrant and holding the suspect for investigation merely to determine if that person has committed some unknown crime.38 However, as with the issuance of an arrest warrant, informants' tips can form the basis for probable cause. (See "Informants' Tips," p. 12.)

PROMPTNESS IN MAKING ARREST WITHOUT WARRANT

An officer's power to arrest without a warrant does not extend to offenses that are long past.39 Therefore, if an officer delays after seeing a crime committed, and then seeks to make the arrest without a warrant, after having had time and opportunity to obtain one, the arrest will be illegal.40 It is not only the officer's right but duty to make such an arrest promptly.[41] Thus, where four months had elapsed since the violation of a municipal ordinance, an attempt to arrest the offender without a warrant was illegal, even though the offense was committed in the officer's presence.[42] Likewise, where an officer saw a crime committed but neglected to make an arrest for several days, an arrest without a warrant was not justified.[43] And even a delay of several hours between the commission of a crime and the arrest without a warrant may make the arrest unlawful.[44] Only when an officer sets out to make an arrest immediately upon seeing an offense, having no time to get a warrant, and then follows up this effort without delay until the offender is apprehended—only then is such an arrest authorized.[45]

ARREST OF FUGITIVES

The rules for arrest without a warrant are not enforced with the same strictness in the case of an escaped convict as in the case of someone who is suspected of crime but has not been arrested or convicted. One reason is that a fugitive, who has been convicted of crime, enjoys no presumption of innocence. On the other hand, a suspect who has not been tried is presumed to be innocent and is entitled to all safeguards for the protection of his or her liberty. Thus, a fugitive, who has no right to be at large, cannot complain if recaptured without a warrant. This is true whether the fugitive's conviction was for a felony or a misdemeanor.[46]

REARREST

When a suspect has been lawfully arrested and escapes from the arresting officer, the suspect may be rearrested without a warrant, regardless of whether the original arrest was with or without a warrant.[47] By escaping, he or she becomes a fugitive from arrest, and any officer can arrest without a warrant "an offender who is endeavoring to escape."[48] Further, since it is a crime to escape from lawful custody,[49] the officer who made the original arrest could rearrest without a warrant for a crime "committed in his presence."[50] (See pp. 20-21 for discussions, "Arrest for Offense Committed in Officer's Presence" and "Arrest When Offender Is Endeavoring to Escape.")

TERRITORIAL EXTENT OF AUTHORITY TO ARREST WITHOUT WARRANT

The general rule in the United States is that police officers have no official power to arrest without a warrant beyond the boundaries of their own jurisdiction.[51] This rule apparently is recognized in Georgia.[52] Thus, officers outside their territorial jurisdiction are viewed simply as private citizens with regard to the authority to make arrests without a warrant.[53] Of course, an officer could arrest legally if the circumstances would justify a private person's making a citizen's arrest. (Citizen's arrest is discussed in the following chapter.)

An exception to the general rule is made when an officer is in **hot pursuit**. Thus, a city policeman who is chasing an offender is not bound to stop at the city limits. The officer may continue pursuit beyond the boundaries of the city and make an arrest outside his or her normal jurisdiction.[54]

Differing from the situation where an officer in fresh pursuit of a fleeing criminal chases the individual across a municipal or county line (intrastate pursuit) is the occasion when the officer must cross a state line in order to make an arrest (interstate pursuit). The arresting powers of the officer in interstate pursuit will vary from state to state and according to whether the offense was a felony or a misdemeanor.[55]

Having no statute dealing specifically with interstate hot pursuit, Georgia follows the traditional common law rule. However, Georgia has by statute[56] adopted a broad policy "to exercise its jurisdiction over crimes and persons charged with the commission of crimes to the fullest extent allowable. . . ."[57] Pursuant to this policy, not only persons who commit an offense "wholly within this state,"[58] but also those who partly commit an offense or engage in an element of an offense while in this state,[59] are subject to prosecution. Further, Georgia claims jurisdiction for any offense committed on any of its boundaries[60] and will proceed to exercise its jurisdiction until ordered to cease by the governor of Georgia.[61] Which county will exercise jurisdiction (venue) is governed by statute.[62]

Despite this broad declaration of jurisdiction, the occasions for pursuit across state lines are numerous and should be approached with caution. Such situations usually do not involve arrest warrants[63] and concern a fresh or hot pursuit—that is, one that is continuous and uninterrupted (although the officer may temporarily lose sight of the suspect).[64] Under the common law rules of arrest, an officer who pursues a suspect of a felony out of the officer's jurisdiction and makes the arrest in another state's territory executes the arrest with the same powers as if the arrest had been made in the state that had granted the officer his or her powers.[65] However, if the suspect who is fleeing is being sought only for a misdemeanor, the powers of the arresting officer are only that of a private citizen in the state of the arrest.[66] To summarize the Georgia common law rule of hot pursuit, *the officer can pursue and arrest a felon across state lines, but not a misdemeanant.*

Some states have adopted the Uniform Fresh Pursuit Act which permits law enforcement officers from other states who enter their state in fresh pursuit to make an arrest.[67] Such a state statute is found in Tennessee:

> Any member of a duly organized state, county, or municipal peace unit of another state of the United States who enters this state in fresh pursuit, and continues within this state in such fresh pursuit of a person in order to arrest him on the ground that he is believed to have committed a felony in such other state, shall have the same authority to arrest and hold such person in custody, as has any member of any duly organized state, county, or municipal law peace unit of this state to arrest and hold in custody a person on the ground that he is believed to have committed a felony in this state.[68]

Thus, Tennessee and Florida,[69] while having adopted the Uniform Act, apply it only to felonies[70] and still follow the common law rule as to misdemeanors.[71]

South Carolina, by case law, allows a private citizen from another state to make an arrest for a felony, but not a misdemeanor.[72]

As was mentioned earlier, an officer who attempts to arrest a misdemeanant who has fled across state lines arrests only with the power of a private citizen. Thus, in Alabama,[73] North Carolina,[74] and Georgia[75] a private citizen may arrest a suspect for a misdemeanor committed in his or her presence. If an officer should, under the circumstances, be required to make an arrest as a private citizen in another state, the officer should immediately deliver the suspect to the local law enforcement officer of the jurisdiction where the arrest occurred. Local officials may detain the suspect for a reasonable time necessary to enable a requisition of the suspect to be made.[76] (See discussion of citizens' arrest for misdemeanors and felonies, pp. 30-31.) Georgia's extradition laws[77] allow for extradition of misdemeanants; however, legal red tape and expense make common use of such process difficult to justify.

Some law enforcement officers, such as conservation rangers, are also deputized federal officers. However, their authority to make arrests across state lines is limited to violations of a federal statute and should not be used to make warrantless interstate arrests for crimes that are only state misdemeanors.

ENDNOTES

1. Thomas v. State, 91 Ga. 204, 206, 18 S.E. 305, 306 (1892); Smith v. State, 84 Ga. App. 79, 82, 65 S.E. 2d 709, 711 (1951).
2. OFFICIAL CODE OF GA. ANN. (O.C.G.A.) §17-4-20.
3. O.C.G.A. §19-13-1.
4. Franklin v. Anderson, 118 Ga. 860, 861-62, 45 S.E. 698, 699 (1903); Savannah News-Press, Inc. v. Harley, 100 Ga. App. 387, 388-89, 111 S.E. 2d 259, 263 (1959).
5. Piedmont Hotel Co. v. Henderson, 9 Ga. App. 672, 680, 72 S.E. 51, 55 (1911).
6. Mullis v. State, 196 Ga. 569, 576, 27 S.E. 2d 91, 97 (1943).
7. Goodwin v. Allen, 89 Ga. App. 187, 189, 78 S.E. 2d 804, 807 (1953); Wilson v. State, 223 Ga. 531, 156 S.E. 2d 446 (1967).
8. Piedmont Hotel Co. v. Henderson, 9 Ga. App. 672, 681, 72 S.E. 51, 55 (1911); Novak v. State, 130 Ga. App. 780, 204 S.E. 2d 491 (1974).
9. Brooks v. State, 114 Ga. 6, 7, 39 S.E. 887, 878 (1901).
10. Ramsey v. State, 92 Ga. 53, 63, 17 S.E. 613, 615 (1893).
11. Shafer v. State, 193 Ga. 748, 754-55, 20 S.E. 2d 34, 38 (1943).
12. Ronemous v. State, 87 Ga. App. 588, 591, 74 S.E. 2d 676, 678 (1953).
13. Pickett v. State, 99 Ga. 12, 15, 25 S.E. 608, 609 (1896).
14. Phelps v. State, 106, Ga. App. 132, 126 S.E. 2d 429, 430 (1962).
15. O.C.G.A. §17-4-23.
16. *Id.*
17. *Id.*
18. Napper v. State, 200 Ga. 626, 629, 38 S.E. 2d 269, 271 (1946); Holmes v. State, 5 Ga. App. 166, 169, 62 S.E. 716, 717-18 (1908).
19. Brooks v. State, 114 Ga. 6, 8, 39 S.E. 877, 878 (1901).
20. Eaker v. State, 4 Ga. App. 649, 652, 62 S.E. 99, 100-101 (1908).
21. Shirley v. City of College Park, 102 Ga. App. 10, 115 S.E. 2d 469, 470 (1960).
22. Napper v. State, 200 Ga. 626, 629, 38 S.E. 2d 269, 271 (1946).
23. O.C.G.A. §19-13-1.
24. *Id.*
25. Croker v. State, 114 Ga. App. 492, 494, 151 S.E. 2d 846, 848 (1966).

28 / ARREST

26. Giddens v. State, 152 Ga. 195, 198-99, 108 S.E. 788, 790 (1921); Michelle v. State, 226 Ga. 450, 175 S.E. 2d 545 (1970).
27. Bloodworth v. State, 113 Ga. App. 278, 147 S.E. 2d 833 (1966); *see also* Mitchell v. State, 226 Ga. 450, 175 S.E. 2d 454 (1970).
28. Douglass v. State, 152 Ga. 379, 391-92, 110 S.E. 168, 174 (1921).
29. *Id.*
30. Savannah News-Press, Inc. v. Harley, 100 Ga. App. 387, 389, 111 S.E. 2d 259, 263 (1959).
31. Cobb v. Bailey, 35 Ga. App. 302, 133 S.E. 42 (1926).
32. *Id.* at 305, 133 S.E. at 43-44.
33. Henry v. United States, 361 U.S. 98, 102 (1959); Johnson v. State, 111 Ga. App. 298, 306, 141 S.E. 2d 574, 581 (1965).
34. Raif v. State, 109 Ga. App. 354, 357, 136 S.E. 2d 169, 172 (1964).
35. Paige v. Potts, 354 F. 2d 212, 213-14 (1965); *see,* Pistor v. State, 219 Ga. 161, 165, 132 S.E. 2d 183, 185 (1963); Creamer v. State, 150 Ga. App. 458, 258 S.E. 2d 212 (1979).
36. Pistor v. State, 219 Ga. 161, 132 S.E. 2d 183 (1963); Raif v. State, 109 Ga. App. 354, 136 S.E. 2d 169 (1964); Harris v. State, 128 Ga. App. 22, 195 S.E. 2d 262 (1973).
37. Richardson v. State, 113 Ga. App. 163, 147 S.E. 2d 653, 654 (1966).
38. Raif v. State, 109 Ga. App. 354, 358, 136 S.E. 2d 169, 172 (1964).
39. *See* Thomas v. State, 91 Ga. 204, 207, 18 S.E. 305, 306 (1892).
40. Reed v. State, 195 Ga. 842, 849, 25 S.E. 2d 692, 697 (1943).
41. *Id.* at 849-50, 25 S.E. 2d at 697; Earl v. State, 124 Ga. 28, 29, 52 S.E. 78, 79 (1905); Yancy v. Fidelity Casualty Co., 96 Ga. App. 476, 100 S.E. 2d 653 (1957).
42. Yates v. State, 127 Ga. 813, 819-20, 56 S.E. 1017, 1019 (1907).
43. Wiggins v. State, 14 Ga. App. 314, 315, 80 S.E. 724 (1914).
44. Yancy v. Fidelity Casualty Co., 96 Ga. App. 476, 478-80, 100 S.E. 2d 653, 655-56 (1957).
45. Yates v. State, 127 Ga. 813, 818, 56 S.E. 1017, 1020 (1907).
46. Williford v. State, 121 Ga. 173, 176-77, 48 S.E. 962, 964 (1904).
47. Maughon v. State, 7 Ga. App. 660, 666, 67 S.E. 842, 845 (1910).
48. *Id.* O.C.G.A. §17-4-20.
49. O.C.G.A. §16-10-52.
50. O.C.G.A. §17-4-20.
51. 5 Am. Jur. 2d *Arrest* §50 (1962); 6 C.J.S. *Arrest* §12b(2) (1937).
52. Blair v. State, 90 Ga. 326, 330, 17 S.E. 96, 97 (1892); *see* Coker v. State, 14 Ga. App. 606, 81 S.E. 818 (1914).
53. Blair v. State, 90 Ga. 326, 330, 17 S.E. 96, 97 (1892).
54. *See* Cantrell v. Mayor & Council of Mt. Airy, 218 Ga. 646, 129 S.E. 2d 910 (1963); Shirley v. City of College Park, 102 Ga. App. 10, 115 S.E. 2d 469 (1960).
55. 5 Am. Jur. 2d *Arrest* §50-51 (1962).
56. O.C.G.A. §17-2-1.
57. LaFave and Scott, *Criminal Law,* pp. 17-18, fn. 3 (1972). Two recognized experts in the area of criminal law have called the above cited Georgia statute a "unique assertion of jurisdiction" in regard to the territorial application of a state's criminal law.

58. O.C.G.A. §17-2-1.
59. *Id.*
60. For a description of the legal boundaries of Georgia, *see* O.C.G.A. §50-2-1 *et seq.*
61. O.C.G.A. §17-2-3.
62. O.C.G.A. §17-2-2.
63. O.C.G.A. §17-4-44. The possession of an arrest warrant would grant no additional power to the officer since the power to serve such a warrant is limited to the boundaries of the state of issuance.
64. Warden v. Hayden, 387 U.S. 294 (1966).
65. 5 Am. Jur. 2d *Arrest* §51 (1962).
66. *Id.*
67. Constitutional Law for Police 2nd ed., Klotter and Kassovitz, (The W.H. Anderson Company, 1968), p. 95.
68. Tenn. Code Ann. §40-7-203 (1982).
69. Fla. Statutes Ann. §941.31 (1968).
70. United States v. Williams, 230 F. Supp. 47, 51 (1961), aff'd 314 F. 2d 795 (6th Cir. 1963).
71. Tarver v. State, 90 Tenn. 485, 16 S.W. 1041 (1891).
72. State v. Whittle, 37 S.E. 923 (S.C. 1901).
73. Code of Ala., 15-10-7 (1975).
74. Gen. Stat. of N. Car. §15A-404.
75. O.C.G.A. §17-2-3.
76. Stalling v. Splain, 253 U.S. 339 (1920).
77. O.C.G.A. §17-13-22. Speaks of extradition for "Treason, felonies or *other crimes.*" Georgia as well as most states has enacted the Uniform Criminal Extradition Act No. 458 (February 21, 1951, [1951] Ga. Laws 726).

4

Arrest by Private Citizens

CRIMES JUSTIFYING CITIZEN'S ARREST

Citizen's Arrest for Misdemeanor

A private citizen who has not been deputized as a peace officer has no authority to make an arrest by service of a warrant,[1] but such citizen may arrest without a warrant any offender who commits a misdemeanor in his or her presence or within his or her immediate knowledge.[2] The terms **in his or her presence** and **within his or her immediate knowledge** mean the same thing, and they are met if, by using any of his or her senses, a citizen has personal knowledge of the commission of an offense.[3] Whether an arrest by a private citizen is lawful depends on whether the offense was committed in his or her presence or within his or her immediate knowledge.[4] Under no other circumstances is a citizen's arrest justified for a crime that amounts only to a misdemeanor. Thus, a private citizen has no authority to make a warrantless arrest for a misdemeanor committed outside of his or her presence or immediate knowledge regardless of whether he or she has time to sue out a warrant or not.[5]

Difficulty arises, however, when someone is arrested while apparently, but not in fact, committing a misdeameanor. In such a situation the arrest may be justified if, under the circumstances, the conduct of the person arrested was sufficient to afford reasonable grounds and probable cause for believing that he or she was violating the law.[6]

Citizen's Arrest for Felony

As in misdemeanor cases, a private citizen may arrest without a warrant any offender who commits a felony in his or her presence or within his or her immediate knowledge.[7] In fact, the Supreme Court of Georgia remarked in an early case that in such a situation a private citizen has not only the right but a duty to apprehend the suspected felon.[8]

A citizen has more powers of arrest in felony cases than in misdemeanor cases. If a suspected felon is escaping or attempting to escape, a citizen may arrest the felon without a warrant, provided the arrest is made on reasonable and probable grounds of suspicion.[9] In addition, the citizen may arrest a suspected felon to prevent a failure of justice for want of a magistrate to issue a warrant. Again, reasonable and probable grounds of suspicion must be present.[10] Finally, a citizen may arrest someone attempting to commit a felony or to prevent the commission of a felony.[11]

An arrest for a felony may sometimes be justified even if the person arrested proves to be innocent.[12] However, an offense must have been committed, and the person making the arrest must have had reasonable and probable grounds for suspecting the guilt of the person arrested.[13]

Citizen's Arrest for Violation of Municipal Ordinance

The right of a private person to arrest does not extend to violators of municipal ordinances. Such violations are regarded by Georgia law neither as felonies nor misdemeanors. Thus, a private person has no authority to take another into custody for spitting on the sidewalk, or for whistling or singing too loudly, or for using a garbage can in violation of municipal regulations. To permit citizens' arrests for violations of mere municipal ordinances, the Supreme Court of Georgia has said, "would be more calculated to produce disorder than to quell it."[14]

PROMPTNESS IN MAKING CITIZEN'S ARREST

A citizen arresting without a warrant for a misdemeanor committed in his or her presence, must do so then and there. If a citizen fails to arrest the offender immediately, the authority to do so is gone.[15] In the case of a felony, however, a citizen may arrest after the commission of the offense, provided the citizen has reasonable and probable grounds to suspect the guilt of the person arrested.[16]

ADDITIONAL AUTHORITY

Authority of Posse Members

Private citizens summoned as members of a posse by a law enforcement officer have the same authority to make arrests as the officer who summoned them. Thus, they can do anything to accomplish the arrest that they could do if they were officers themselves.[17] (See "Summoning Assistance: Posse," p. 38, for a further discussion.)

Citizens are encouraged, but not required, to go to the aid of law enforcement officers, particularly when their lives are endangered or they are hindered in the performance of their duties. Such citizens are immune, to the same extent as the officer, from any criminal liability which might otherwise be imposed as a result of their effort to give assistance.[18]

Authority of Bondsmen

When one accused of crime is released on bond, he or she is not entirely free but is simply transferred from the custody of the sheriff or other official to the custody of the bondsman. If the accused subsequently fails to appear, the bondsman may seize the accused in order to make delivery in discharge of the bond. Rearrest by the bondsman is not dependent on procuring a warrant nor is it limited by state boundaries.[19] A bondsman, unable to apprehend the accused, may designate someone else to do so and to deliver the accused to the sheriff.[20]

Authority of Hospital Staff Regarding Tuberculosis Patients

If a voluntary tuberculosis patient becomes intoxicated and unruly on hospital grounds, he or she may be taken into custody by hospital personnel, isolated, and held for trial.[21] This action would constitute an arrest without a warrant under the Code.[22] This statute makes being intoxicated on hospital grounds by a tuberculosis patient a misdemeanor. If such a person is taken into custody under this provision, he or she must, within 48 hours of the arrest, be brought before an officer authorized to receive an affidavit and to issue a warrant.[23]

DUTY UPON MAKING CITIZEN'S ARREST

When a citizen's arrest is made, the apprehension is for the sole purpose of taking the accused before an official authorized to take affidavits and issue warrants.[24] This must be done within 48 hours by the person who made the arrest.[25] It is not enough, therefore, simply to turn the person arrested over to a police officer who has no authority to take an affidavit and issue a warrant.[26]

The person arrested may be detained for a reasonable time necessary to obtain a warrant, but imprisonment beyond a reasonable time is illegal. What constitutes a reasonable time is a question of fact, depends upon the circumstances, and is for a jury to decide.[27]

ENDNOTES

1. Coleman v. State, 121 Ga. 594, 49 S.E. 716 (1905).
2. OFFICIAL CODE OF GA. ANN. (O.C.G.A.) §17-4-60.
3. Piedmont Hotel Co. v. Henderson, 9 Ga. App. 672, 681, 72 S.E. 51, 55 (1911); Novak v. State, 130 Ga. App. 780, 204 S.E. 2d 491 (1974); Forchard v. State, 130 Ga. App. 801, 204 S.E. 2d 516 (1974); Johnson v. Jackson, 140 Ga. App. 252, 230 S.E. 2d 756 (1976).
4. Walker v. State, 44 Ga. App. 838, 242 S.E. 2d 753 (1978).
5. Delegal v. State, 109 Ga. 518, 521-22, 35 S.E. 105, 106 (1900).
6. Southern Ry. v. Gresham, 114 Ga. 183, 184, 39 S.E. 883 (1901); *contra,* Walker v. State, 46 Ga. App. 824, 828, 169 S.E. 315, 317 (1933).
7. O.C.G.A. §17-4-60.
8. Long v. State, 12 Ga. 293, 318 (1852); Johnson v. Jackson, 140 Ga. App. 252, 230 S.E. 2d 756 (1976).
9. O.C.G.A. §17-4-60; Harper v. State, 129 Ga. 770, 59 S.E. 792 (1907).
10. Croom v. State, 85 Ga. 718, 723, 11 S.E. 1035, 1037 (1890).
11. Cobb v. Bailey, 35 Ga. App. 302, 305, 133 S.E. 42, 44 (1926); Johnson v. Jackson, 140 Ga. App. 252, 230 S.E. 2d 756 (1976).
12. *See* Habersham v. State, 56 Ga. 62 (1876). *But see* Walker v. State, 46 Ga. App. 824, 169 S.E. 315 (1933).
13. Long v. State, 12 Ga. 293, 318 (1852); Annot., 133 A.L.R. 608, 613 (1941).
14. Graham v. State, 143 Ga. 440, 444-45, 85 S.E. 328, 330 (1915).
15. Delegal v. State, 109 Ga. 518, 522, 35 S.E. 105, 106-107 (1900); McWilliams v. Interstate Bakeries, Inc., 439 F. 2d 16 (5th Cir., 1971).
16. *See* Snelling v. State, 87 Ga. 50, 13 S.E. 154 (1891); Croom v. State, 85 Ga. 718, 11 S.E. 1035 (1890).
17. Robinson v. State, 93 Ga. 77, 83, 18 S.E. 1018, 1019 (1893).
18. O.C.G.A. §16-3-22.
19. 8 Am. Jur. 2d *Bail and Recognizance* §117 (1963).
20. Coleman v. State, 121 Ga. 594, 597, 49 S.E. 716, 717 (1905).
21. O.C.G.A. §31-14-13.
22. O.C.G.A. §17-4-20.
23. 1972 Op. Att'y Gen. U72-106.
24. O.C.G.A. §17-4-62; Croker v. State, 114 Ga. App. 492, 494, 151 S.E. 2d 846, 848 (1966).

25. O.C.G.A. §17-4-62.
26. Ocean S.S. Co. v. Williams, 69 Ga. 251, 262-63 (1882).
27. O.C.G.A. §17-4-62; Habersham v. State, 56 Ga. 61 (1876); Dukes v. State, 109 Ga. App. 825, 137 S.E. 2d 532 (1964).

5

Procedure When Making Arrest

POSSESSION OF WARRANT AT TIME OF ARREST

When a lawful arrest cannot be made except under a warrant, the arresting officer should have the warrant in his or her physical possession at the time of the arrest, or so near at hand that it can be exhibited upon demand.[1] As a general rule, it is not enough that a warrant has, in fact, been issued. Unless the arresting officer is in possession of it or can display it upon demand, he or she derives no authority from it.[2] Accordingly, the arresting officer has no authority to take the person sought into custody when the warrant is at the officer's home some distance from the scene of arrest,[3] in another town in a distant part of the county,[4] or simply retained by one officer who sends another to make the arrest.[5]

This general rule may be relaxed somewhat in the case of felonies, and, of course, it does not apply to situations where an arrest could be made with or without a warrant. If an officer could arrest without a warrant — to prevent a suspected felon from escaping, for example — the fact that a warrant had been issued, but was not in the officer's actual possession, would be of no consequence.[6]

When two or more officers go together to make an arrest, a warrant obviously can be in the physical possession of only one of them. In this situation a valid arrest can be made by an officer who does not have the warrant, provided it is in the possession of another officer who is in the same neighborhood and with whom he or she is acting in concert.[7] Similarly, a person summoned as a member of a posse may make an arrest without having physical possession of the warrant, if in the same neighborhood as the officer who does and if acting under the officer's direction.[8]

GIVING NOTICE OF AUTHORITY

Generally, a person about to be arrested has the right to know that he or she is being taken into custody by one with lawful authority.[9] Therefore, it is the duty of an officer who attempts to make an arrest to identify him- or herself[10] and, if the arrest is made under a warrant, to exhibit it.[11] Of course, a suspect cannot complain of nonproduction of a warrant where the suspect's own conduct — violent resistance, for example — prevents it.[12]

If the person sought demands to see evidence of the officer's authority, the officer must show it.[13] If, however, the officer is known to the suspect as an officer, there is no obligation to exhibit his or her authority until after the suspect has submitted to arrest.[14] Notice of the official character of someone making an arrest may be expressed or implied.[15]

The suspect may have notice if he or she

- actually knows that the person making an arrest is an officer,
- sees the officer's uniform or badge,
- is apprehended while committing a crime,
- is pursued from the scene of a crime, or
- is told by the officer that an arrest is being made and why.[16]

The residents of an officer's territorial jurisdiction ordinarily are presumed to be aware of the officer's official character; however, the person arrested or whose arrest was attempted may overcome this presumption with proof to the contrary.[17]

If an officer who is not known to a suspect fails to present identification in some way or to make his or her purpose known, the suspect has the right to resist what appears to the suspect to be an unjustifed assault.[18] (Justified resistance is discussed on p. 39.) Such failure places the officer in the position of a private person attempting an arrest; the officer has no authority to act on the warrant until manifesting some notice of his or her official character.[19]

USE OF FORCE

An officer making a lawful arrest has the right to use whatever force is reasonably necessary to accomplish the arrest,[20] but no more.[21] The use of unnecessary force or violence will constitute an assault against the person arrested and will justify the person's using force against the officer in self-defense.[22] (Justified resistance is discussed on p. 39.)

The degree of force that is reasonable depends upon the seriousness of the crime and the sort of resistance offered. In all cases, an officer may defend him- or herself with whatever force is necessary. The officer cannot, however, in the guise of self-defense, mistreat a suspect needlessly. For example, if slight resistance is offered, an officer has no right to beat the accused violently in the face with a cane.[23] Likewise, an officer cannot punish a suspect simply for being insolent or using abusive language,[24] although a case may be made against the suspect for such conduct, provided the language in question is so abusive as to constitute "fighting words."[25]

SHOOTING OR KILLING TO PREVENT ESCAPE

If the person sought to be arrested makes no effort to resist arrest but only seeks to avoid it by flight, an officer generally cannot shoot or kill the person.[26] Such, at least, is the case if the offense is either a misdemeanor[27] or the violation of a municipal ordinance,[28] even if the officer cannot otherwise make the arrest. In a misdemeanor case, an officer is justified in shooting only if the person sought to be arrested tries to harm the officer; that is, the officer can act in self-defense.[29]

Where the offense is a felony, however, greater force may be used to prevent an escape, even to the extent of slaying the offender where there are sufficient circumstances.[30] What constitutes "sufficient circumstances" is not clear, but if an arrest can be made without killing the accused, killing the accused would probably be murder or manslaughter.[31]

The use of deadly force to prevent escape can be a serious problem. The Supreme Court has ruled that a Tennessee statute permitting police to use deadly force to prevent escape of suspected felons violates Fourth Amendment prohibitions against unreasonable seizures insofar as it authorizes the use of such force against apparently unarmed, nondangerous suspects. The court further stated that such force may not be used unless it is necessary to prevent escape and the officer has probable cause to believe that the suspect poses a significant threat of death or serious physical injury to the officer or others (i.e., armed and dangerous).[32]

ENTERING PRIVATE PREMISES

An officer's right to arrest for criminal offense generally includes the right to enter private premises to make the arrest. Thus, an officer seeking to execute a warrant is authorized by statute to break open the door of any house where the offender is concealed but should only do so when he or she cannot otherwise gain admittance.[33] An officer may not enter a private dwelling to make a warrantless arrest for a routine felony.[34] Either consent of the person to be arrested or exigent circumstances must be present. Mere probable cause is insufficient. However, if the suspect can be induced to come outside, he or she may be arrested.[35] These powers are applicable in the nighttime as well as during the day.[36] However, before entering a private dwelling an officer generally should announce the purpose and demand entrance.[37]

Apparently, a private person also may enter a private dwelling to apprehend an offender when justified in making a citizen's arrest.[38]

STOPPING TRAIN

A law enforcement officer has authority to stop a train to arrest someone on it. The officer also may stop the train to remove the prisoner after making the arrest.[39]

SUMMONING ASSISTANCE: POSSE

When making arrests, law enforcement officers may summon other officers[40] or private citizens[41] to their assistance. When an arresting officer calls to a fellow officer for aid, it is the duty of the second officer to respond.[42] Private citizens have a similar duty to assist a known police officer,[43] although there apparently is no penalty for refusing.

Officers may call citizens either verbally or in writing to assist them,[44] but this does not make such citizens deputies or officers.[45] Neither, however, are they mere private persons; their true legal position is what is called a **posse comitatus**.[46] Posse members may include law enforcement officers such as city police officers summoned beyond their own territorial jurisdiction by a sheriff.[47]

The law grants to posse members the same protection in making arrests as the officer who summoned them.[48] Thus, posse members may perform any act to promote or accomplish the arrest which they could perform if they were law enforcement officers. In order to have the benefit of this protection, it is not essential that posse members remain in the actual physical presence of the officer who summoned them. It is sufficient if they are in the same neighborhood, acting under the officer's command and in concert with the officer in an attempt to make the arrest.[49]

WHEN RESISTANCE IS JUSTIFIED

The law places upon every citizen the duty to submit quietly to a lawful arrest.[50] However, an illegal attempt to take a person into custody is an assault, and the person sought to be arrested may use as much force as necessary to repel the assault and avoid the arrest.[51] This is true whether the illegal arrest is attempted by a law enforcement officer or a private citizen.[52] However, the assumption that the arrest is unlawful is made at the peril of the person who resists.[53]

One who resists an illegal arrest is not required to flee if by flight he or she could avoid being taken into custody.[54] But while this person may stand firm he or she may use only such force in resisting as is necessary, and is accountable for any excess.[55] Resistance to the point of killing, for example, while sometimes justified,[56] more often results in a charge of manslaughter or even murder against the person resisting the unlawful arrest.[57]

Although one is not bound to submit to illegal arrest, resistance must be in good faith. Thus, a person who knows or believes that the arrest is lawful, has a duty to submit quietly to custody.[58]

ENDNOTES

1. Adams v. State 121 Ga. 163(3), 48 S.E. 910 (1904); Croker v. State, 114 Ga. App. 492, 494, 151 S.E. 2d 846, 847 (1966).
2. Giddens v. State, 154 Ga. 54, 60-61, 113 S.E. 386, 389 (1922).
3. Adams v. State 121 Ga. 163, 165, 48 S.E. 910, 911 (1904).
4. Giddens v. State, 154 Ga. 54, 60-61, 113 S.E. 386, 389 (1922); Jones v. State, 114 Ga. 73, 74, 39 S.E. 861 (1901).
5. Jones v. State, 114 Ga. 73, 74, 39 S.E. 861 (1901).
6. Croker v. State, 114 Ga. App. 492, 494, 151 S.E. 2d 846, 848 (1966).
7. Adams v. State, 121 Ga. 163, 165, 48 S.E. 910, 911 (1904).
8. Robinson v. State, 93 Ga. 77, 83-85, 18 S.E. 1018, 1019 (1893). For a further discussion of the posse, see "Authority of Posse Members," p. 32, "Summoning Assistance: Posse," p. 38.

40 / ARREST

9. Graham v. State, 143 Ga. 440, 445, 85 S.E. 328, 331 (1915).
10. Morton v. State, 190 Ga. 792, 799, 10 S.E. 2d 836, 840 (1940); Douglass v. State, 152 Ga. 379, 392, 110 S.E. 168, 174 (1921).
11. Jones v. State, 114 Ga. 73, 74, 39 S.E. 861 (1901); Davis v. State, 79 Ga. 767, 768-69, 4 S.E. 318 (1887).
12. Robinson v. State, 93 Ga. 77, 88-89, 18 S.E. 1018, 1020 (1893).
13. *See* Jones v. State, 114 Ga. 73, 74, 39 S.E. 861 (1901); Robinson v. State, 93 Ga. 77, 88-89, 18 S.E. 1018, 1020 (1893).
14. Robinson v. State, 93 Ga. 77, 88, 18 S.E. 1018, 1020 (1893).
15. Graham v. State, 143 Ga. 440, 445, 85 S.E. 328, 331 (1915).
16. Franklin v. Anderson, 118 Ga. 860, 863, 45 S.E. 698, 700 (1903).
17. Croom v. State, 85 Ga. 718, 724, 11 S.E. 1035, 1037 (1890).
18. Franklin v. Anderson, 118 Ga. 860, 863, 45 S.E. 698, 700 (1903).
19. Franklin v. Anderson, 118 Ga. 860, 45 S.E. 698 (1903).
20. Morton v. State, 190 Ga. 792, 799, 10 S.E. 2d 836, 841 (1940); Ramsey v. State, 92 Ga. 53, 63-64, 17 S.E. 613, 615 (1893).
21. Mullis v. State, 196 Ga. 569, 577-78, 27 S.E. 2d 91, 98 (1943).
22. Napper v. State, 200 Ga. 626, 629, 38 S.E. 2d 269, 271 (1946).
23. Moody v. State, 120 Ga. 868, 48 S.E. 340 (1904).
24. *Id.* at 869, 48 S.E. at 341; Dixon v. State, 12 Ga. App. 17, 18, 76 S.E. 794, 795 (1912).
25. OFFICIAL CODE OF GA. ANN. (O.C.G.A.) §16-11-39.
26. McAllister v. State, 7 Ga. App. 541, 67 S.E. 221 (1910).
27. Savannah News-Press, Inc. v. Harley, 100 Ga. App. 387, 389, 111 S.E. 2d 259, 263 (1959).
28. Holmes v. State, 5 Ga. App. 166, 170, 62 S.E. 716, 718 (1908).
29. Eaton v. State, 83 Ga. App. 82, 85, 62 S.E. 2d 677, 679 (1950).
30. Mullis v. State, 196 Ga. 569, 578, 27 S.E. 2d 91, 98 (1943).
31. Dover v. State, 109 Ga. 485, 488, 34 S.E. 1030, 1031 (1900).
32. Tennessee v. Garner, 105 Sup. Ct. 1694 (1985).
33. O.C.G.A. §17-4-3.
34. Payton v. New York, 445 U.S. 573, 576 (1980).
35. Mincey v. State, 251 Ga. 255, 261, 304 S.E. 2d 882, 888 (1983).
36. Groves v. State, 175 Ga. 37, 41, 164 S.E. 822, 824 (1932).
37. *Id.;* Miller v. United States, 357 U.S. 301 (1958).
38. Snelling v. State, 87 Ga. 50, 13 S.E. 154 (1891).
39. Brunswick & Western R.R. v. Ponder, 117 Ga. 63, 66, 43 S.E. 430, 431 (1903).
40. Harrell v. State, 75 Ga. 842, 846 (1885); O.C.G.A. §17-4-24.
41. O.C.G.A. §17-4-24.
42. Harrell v. State, 75 Ga. 842, 846 (1885).
43. *See* Robinson v. State, 93 Ga. 77, 83, 18 S.E. 1018, 1019 (1893); Annot., 29 A.L.R. 2d 825, 826 (1953); O.C.G.A. §16-3-22.
44. O.C.G.A. §17-4-24.
45. Robinson v. State, 93 Ga. 77, 83, 18 S.E. 1018, 1019 (1893).
46. *Id.*
47. Phillips v. State, 66 Ga. 755 (1881).

48. O.C.G.A. §16-3-22.
49. Robinson v. State, 93 Ga. 77, 83-84, 18 S.E. 1018, 1019 (1893).
50. Ramsey v. State, 92 Ga. 53, 17 S.E. 613 (1893).
51. Napper v. State, 200 Ga. 626, 629, 38 S.E. 2d 269, 271 (1946).
52. Holmes v. State, 5 Ga. App. 166, 62 S.E. 716 (1908).
53. Dixon v. State, 12 Ga. App. 17, 18, 76 S.E. 794, 794-95 (1912); *see* Williams v. State, 148 Ga. 310, 96 S.E. 385 (1918).
54. Faulkner v. State, 166 Ga. 645, 663, 144 S.E. 193, 201 (1928).
55. Napper v. State, 200 Ga. 626, 629, 38 S.E. 2d 269, 271 (1946).
56. Holmes v. State, 5 Ga. App. 166, 168-69, 62 S.E. 716, 717 (1908).
57. Graham v. State, 143 Ga. 440, 446, 85 S.E. 328, 331 (1915); Thomas v. State, 91 Ga. 204, 206, 18 S.E. 305 (1892).
58. Mullis v. State, 196 Ga. 569, 577, 27 S.E. 2d 91, 98 (1943).

6

Rights and Duties after Making Arrest

DUTIES TO ARRESTEES

Advising Person Arrested of Constitutional Rights

Every person taken into police custody is guaranteed certain rights by the Constitution of the United States. Violation of these rights can result in a confession or other evidence later being inadmissible in a trial. Therefore, an arresting officer must advise the prisoner of these rights before the prisoner is questioned or makes any statement to the police.

Specifically, a person arrested for crime must be warned of the right to remain silent; that any statement a prisoner makes can and will be used as evidence against him or her in a court of law; and that the prisoner has the right to consult with an attorney, either self-retained or court-appointed, and to have the attorney present during interrogation. These rights may be waived by a prisoner, but no waiver is effective unless it is given intelligently, knowingly, and voluntarily without any trickery or duress by the police.[1]

Some police departments furnish their officers with reminders that warnings must be given. A pocket-sized card prepared by the District Attorney's Association of Georgia is representative (see Figure 3, p. 43).

If the suspect indicates in any manner, prior to or during questioning, the wish to remain silent or to consult with an attorney, the interrogation must cease, unless permission is given by the attorney.

Care of Property Found in Possession of Person Arrested

Under some circumstances, such as when someone arrested is too intoxicated to care for his or her personal belongings, it is the duty of the arresting officer to take charge of them for safekeeping and to return them at a later date.[2]

RIGHT TO SEARCH INCIDENT TO LAWFUL ARREST

This subject is treated in *Part II, Search and Seizure,* beginning on p. 74.

COMMITMENT HEARINGS

Right to Commitment Hearing

Every person arrested for a crime is entitled to a prompt commitment hearing at which the state must show that there is probable cause to believe the person guilty of the offense charged.[3] The purpose of the hearing is not to settle the question of guilt or innocence,[4] but to determine whether the person arrested should be held so that a grand jury can indict or refuse to indict him for the crime charged.[5]

Figure 3. *Miranda Warning*

1. You have the right to remain silent.
2. Anything you say can and will be used against you in a court of law.
3. You have the right to talk to a lawyer and have him present with you while you are being questioned.
4. If you cannot afford to hire a lawyer, one will be appointed to represent you before any questioning, if you wish.
5. You can decide at any time to exercise these rights and not answer any questions or make any statements.

Waiver

After the warning and in order to secure a waiver, the following questions should be asked and an affirmative reply secured to each question.

1. Do you understand each of these rights I have explained to you?
2. Having these rights in mind, do you wish to talk to us now?

The accused may choose to waive the right to a commitment hearing.[6] Waiver must be given freely, however, and if obtained under duress will not be valid.[7] Since the commitment hearing is preliminary in nature and not a required step in a felony prosecution, its absence will not be considered reversible error on appeal.[8]

In regard to a commitment hearing, it should be noted that a court of criminal jurisdiction is not required to inquire as to how a defendant is brought before it.[9] Thus, the fact that the arrest may be illegal, or that it was or was not effected by a lawful officer, does not preclude trial of the accused.[10]

Who May Hold Commitment Hearing?

Commitment hearings may be held by judges of superior courts, judges of state courts, judges of probate courts, magistrates, or officers of any municipality who have the criminal jurisdiction of a magistrate.[11] In addition, they may be held by the judges of police and recorder's courts and by mayors and other officials who preside over the courts of municipal corporations.[12]

Normally a prisoner should be taken before the most convenient and accessible judicial officer who has authority to hear the case.[13] Except in the case of a "special warrant," any judicial officer of the county in which the crime is alleged to have been committed has such authority.[14] (For an explaination of "special warrant," see "Where Warrants Are Returnable," p. 17.) However, if the prisoner objects to the magistrate selected, the arresting officer must carry the prisoner before some other judicial officer, provided there is no suspicion of an improper motive. In no case, however, has a prisoner the right to select the magistrate who presides at the hearing.[15]

Commitment Hearing for Person Arrested under Warrant

When an arrest is made under a warrant, the arresting officer is required by statute to take the prisoner, with the warrant, before a committing officer within 72 hours.[16] The arresting officer also must notify the accused before the hearing when and where it will be held; otherwise the prisoner must be released.[17] The accused may be imprisoned for a reasonable time before seeing a magistrate if such action is necessary.[18] Imprisonment beyond a reasonable time, however, is unlawful, and the officer responsible may be guilty of false imprisonment.[19] What constitutes a reasonable time is a question to be determined by a jury.[20]

The 72-hour requirement may be satisfied even when a hearing is not held within that time. It is sufficient if the accused simply appears within 72 hours before a committing magistrate; the hearing then may be set for a later time.[21] It is also permissible for the prisoner to be taken before the magistrate by an officer other than the one who made the arrest.[22] Furthermore, the accused may not complain of any delay caused by his or her own actions.[23]

Both the 72-hour requirement and the notice requirement have been criticized by the Supreme Court of Georgia as being vague, uncertain, and indefinite. For example, no penalty is imposed if the arresting officer fails to take the prisoner before a magistrate within 72 hours, nor is the prisoner entitled by statute to release if a hearing is not held within that time. Furthermore, the statute does not indicate when or how a prisoner is to be notified of his hearing, other than to say that notice must be given before the hearing.[24]

Both requirements become unnecessary if the prisoner is indicted before the 72-hour period expires. The prisoner is then held by virtue of the indictment rather than under the warrant.[25]

Commitment Hearing for Person Arrested without Warrant

When an arrest is made without a warrant, the arresting officer is required by statute to take his or her prisoner before a magistrate within 48 hours and obtain a warrant; otherwise, the prisoner must be released.[26] This release, however, is only until a warrant can be obtained and does not mean that the defendant cannot be rearrested.[27] The accused may be imprisoned for a reasonable time before seeing a magistrate.[28] However, imprisonment beyond a reasonable time is illegal, and the officer responsible may be guilty of false imprisonment.[29] What is a reasonable time is a jury question and may well be less than 48 hours, which is the outer limit of reasonableness.[30]

ACCEPTING BAIL

Every person accused of a crime less than a capital felony is entitled, as a matter of right, to give bail before indictment and trial.[31] Bail ordinarily is accepted by the judge of the committing court or some other authorized judicial officer.[32] In misdemeanor cases, however, sheriffs and constables are authorized to accept bail in reasonable amounts, provided the sureties offered are approved by a sheriff of any county.33 Such bail may not be accepted in a county other than that in which the offense is alleged to have been committed.34

KEEPING RECORDS

All sheriffs, chiefs of police, and heads of other law enforcement agencies are required by law to maintain records on all persons arrested by their officers and charged with crime. The records must include the name, address, and age of every person arrested and must be open for public inspection unless otherwise provided by law.35

ENDNOTES

1. Miranda v. Arizona, 384 U.S. 436 (1966).
2. Connolly v. Thurber Whyland Co., 92 Ga. 651, 654, 18 S.E. 1004, 1005 (1893); Garner v. State, 154 Ga. App. 101, 267 S.E. 2d 823 (1980).
3. OFFICIAL CODE OF GA. ANN. (O.C.G.A.) §17-4-26.
4. Savannah News-Press, Inc. v. Harley, 100 Ga. App. 387, 391, 111 S.E. 2d 259, 264 (1959).
5. Cannon v. Grimes, 223 Ga. 35, 36, 153 S.E. 2d 445, 446 (1967).
6. O.C.G.A. §17-6-16.
7. Id.
8. State v. Middlebrooks, 236 Ga. 52, 222 S.E. 2d 343 (1976).
9. Joiner v. State, 66 Ga. App. 106, 17 S.E. 2d 101 (1941); Nobles v. State, 81 Ga. App. 229, 58 S.E. 2d 496 (1950).
10. Mitchell v. State, 126 Ga. 84, 54 S.E. 931 (1906).
11. O.C.G.A. §17-7-20.
12. O.C.G.A. §§17-7-22, 36-32-3.
13. O.C.G.A. §17-4-21.
14. O.C.G.A. §17-4-25.
15. O.C.G.A. §17-4-21.
16. O.C.G.A. §17-4-26.
17. Id.
18. Moses v. State, 6 Ga. App. 251, 253, 64 S.E. 699 (1909).
19. Stone v. National Surety Corp., 57 Ga. App. 427, 195 S.E. 905 (1938).
20. Piedmont Hotel Co. v. Henderson, 9 Ga. App. 672, 682, 72 S.E. 51, 56 (1911).
21. Whitfield v. State, 115 Ga. App. 231, 232, 154 S.E. 2d 294, 296 (1967).
22. French v. State, 99 Ga. App. 149, 152, 107 S.E. 2d 890, 894 (1959).
23. Blocker v. Clark, 126 Ga. 484, 490, 54 S.E. 1022, 1024 (1906).
24. Pennaman v. Walton, 220 Ga. 295, 297-98, 138 S.E. 2d 571, 572-73 (1964).
25. Whisman v. State, 223 Ga. 124, 153 S.E. 2d 548 (1967).
26. O.C.G.A. §17-4-62, applied in, Blake v. State 109 Ga. App. 636, 642, 137 S.E. 2d 49, 53 (1964).

27. Blake v. State, 109 Ga. App. 636, 641, 137 S.E. 2d 49, 53 (1964); Middlebrooks v. State, 135 Ga. App. 411, 218 S.E. 2d 110 (1975) rev'd. on other grounds, 236 Ga. 52, 222 S.E. 2d 343 (1976).
28. O.C.G.A. §17-4-62, applied in, Dukes v. State, 109 Ga. App. 825, 826, 137 S.E. 2d 532, 534 (1964).
29. Stone v. National Surety Corp., 57 Ga. App. 427, 195 S.E. 905 (1938).
30. Dukes v. State, 109 Ga. App. 825, 826, 137 S.E. 2d 532, 534 (1964).
31. O.C.G.A. §17-6-1; Newsome v. Scott, 151 Ga. 639, 107 S.E. 854 (1921).
32. O.C.G.A. §17-6-1.
33. O.C.G.A. §17-6-2.
34. Lamb v. Dillard, 94 Ga. 206, 208, 21 S.E. 463, 464 (1894).
35. O.C.G.A. §17-4-27.

Immunity from Criminal Arrest

WHO ENJOYS IMMUNITY FROM CRIMINAL ARREST?

Foreign Representatives

Immunity or freedom from criminal arrest, as opposed to arrest in civil cases, is enjoyed only by certain representatives of foreign countries such as ambassadors and ministers.[1] All other persons who violate the criminal laws of Georgia are subject to arrest.

LIMITED IMMUNITY FROM CRIMINAL ARREST

Members of Congress

The Constitution of the United States exempts U.S. senators and representatives from arrest while attending Congress and on their way to and from sessions of Congress, except in cases of "treason, felony or breach of the peace."[2] These terms have been interpreted by the U.S. Supreme Court to embrace all criminal offenses.[3] The effect is that members of Congress may be arrested for the violation of any criminal statute.

Members of the General Assembly

Members of the Georgia legislature enjoy a freedom from arrest similar to that extended to members of Congress. They are exempt from arrest while attending the General Assembly and on their way to and from sessions of the legislature, except in cases of "treason, felony, larceny or breach of the peace."[4] Although these terms have not been interpreted by the Supreme Court of Georgia, their effect probably is to leave legislators liable to arrest for the violation of criminal statutes.

IMMUNITY FROM ARREST IN CIVIL CASES

Who Is Exempt?

Various other groups are extended immunity from arrest in civil cases, but their immunity does not extend to criminal arrests. They include members of the state militia during the performance of their duties[5] and witnesses on their way to and from court,[6] among others.[7]

ENDNOTES

1. 4 Am. Jur. 2d *Ambassadors and Consuls* §9 (1962); Annot., 1 A.L.R. 1159 (1919).
2. U.S. Const. art. I, sec. 6.
3. Williamson v. United States, 207 U.S. 425, 444-46 (1908).
4. Ga. Const. art. III, sec. IV, par. IX; OFFICIAL CODE OF GA. ANN. (O.C.G.A.) §17-4-1.
5. O.C.G.A. §17-4-2.
6. O.C.G.A. §24-10-1; Turner v. McGee, 217 Ga. 769, 773, 125 S.E. 2d 36, 39 (1962).
7. 5 Am. Jur. 2d *Arrest* §§102-111 (1962).

Liability and Jurisdiction of Law Enforcement Officers

OFFICER LIABILITY

The law enforcement officer making a warrantless arrest without probable cause and with malice does so at his or her own risk.[1] The law defines malice as an act done with "personal spite or general disregard of right consideration of mankind, directed by chance against the person injured."[2] This means that an officer who makes a warrantless arrest without probable cause and with spite towards the arrestee or in callous disregard of the arrestee's due process rights is subject to liability through a civil suit that can be filed by the arrestee. By inference, then, an arrest made in good faith with a warrant or with probable cause would not subject the officer to any civil liability.

OFFICER JURISDICTION

Georgia State Patrol

The criminal jurisdiction of the state patrol extends throughout Georgia,[3] and patrol officers ordinarily make arrests for offenses arising from the violation of traffic laws or of laws regulating the use, ownership, and control of motor vehicles, or for offenses committed on the highways.[4] They also may arrest fugitives,[5] however, and the patrol may at times be ordered to assist local law enforcement officers, in which case patrol officers are authorized to make arrests for violations of all criminal laws.[6]

In addition, the state patrol is authorized to enforce the criminal laws of Georgia on state property and arrest persons violating these laws.[7]

Georgia Bureau of Investigation

The criminal jurisdiction of the Georgia Bureau of Investigation (GBI) extends throughout Georgia, and the arrest powers of its agents are the same as those of the state patrol (see preceding section).[8]

City Police

City police departments generally have official authority only within the geographical boundaries of their own city or town,[9] unless in hot pursuit of an offender.[10] However, they may also be granted authority over municipal airports located outside the city limits.[11]

Sheriffs

A sheriff is regarded as "a conservator of peace" within his or her county,[12] and accordingly has criminal jurisdiction that is generally limited to the county's geographical boundaries. However, the sheriff may travel outside the county to execute arrest warrants,[13] and presumably has authority beyond the county when in hot pursuit of an offender.

County Police

County police departments generally are limited in their criminal jurisdiction to the geographical boundaries of their own county.[14] However, they also may be granted authority over airports established by their county but within the boundaries of another county.[15] Presumably, county police officers could arrest in their official capacity if hot pursuit of an offender took them beyond their county boundaries.

Marshals

Marshals are municipal police officers[16] whose criminal jurisdiction is the same as that of city or town police officers (see above).

Coroners

A coroner of a county is authorized to execute warrants when the sheriff of the same county is disqualified or when the sheriff or sheriff's deputies refuse to execute such warrants.[17] The coroner's jurisdiction in such a situation presumably is the same as that of the sheriff (see above).

State Revenue Agents

State revenue agents have statewide authority to execute arrest warrants and under certain circumstances to arrest without warrants for violations of the laws regarding the manufacture, transportation, distribution, sale, storage, or possession of liquor, beer, or wine. When directed by the governor or requested by municipal authorities, the State Revenue Commissioner may order special agents and enforcement officers to render assistance in any criminal matter.[18]

Prison Guards, Wardens, and Correctional Officers

State law gives to the following—the wardens, deputies, and/or assistants; superintendents, deputies, and/or assistants; and correctional officers of any state or county institutions operated under the jurisdiction of the State Board of Offender Rehabilitation—all the power and authority granted to state law enforcement officers by the legislature. These powers include, but are not limited to, the authority to make arrests for violations of criminal laws in accordance with rules and regulations promulgated by the board and the power to carry weapons.[19]

State Conservation Rangers

State conservation rangers have the power and authority to enforce any state law

1. on all property owned or controlled by the Department of Natural Resources;
2. pertaining to functions assigned to that department;
3. when its violation is in conjunction with the violation of a state law relating to Department of Natural Resources' functions;
4. when ordered to do so by the governor;
5. to protect any life or property when the circumstances demand action; and
6. to assist in the enforcement of state law when so requested by the Georgia Bureau of Investigation or the Department of Public Safety.[20]

State Probation Officers

State probation officers may arrest without a warrant probationers under their supervision who have violated probation in a material respect.[21] State probation officers may do this anywhere in the state.

State Drug Inspectors

State drug inspectors have the authority to arrest persons violating the provisions of the Georgia Controlled Substances

Act[22] and the Dangerous Drug Act,[23] and to seize all articles declared to be contraband under the provisions of these acts.[24]

State Fire Marshal

The State Fire Marshal and deputies are authorized to make arrests in the enforcement of state arson statutes.[25]

Executive Security Guards

Security guards employed by the Security Guard Division of the Department of Public Safety have the power to arrest in their duties of protecting the governor, lieutenant governor, Speaker of the House, and their families.[26]

Janitors and Guards of Public Buildings

Janitors and watchmen employed by the keeper of public buildings and grounds are authorized to make arrests to prevent the abuse of the buildings and to suppress disorderly conduct therein.[27]

Department of Human Resources Institutional Police

Police at the facilities and institutions under the supervision and administrative control of the Department of Human Resources are empowered to make arrests on the grounds or in the buildings of these facilities.[28]

Campus Police

The campus police and other security personnel of the University System of Georgia, who are regular employees of the University System of Georgia, have arrest power for offenses committed upon any property or within 500 yards of property under the jurisdiction of the Board of Regents of the University System of Georgia.[29]

ENDNOTES
1. OFFICIAL CODE OF GA. ANN. (O.C.G.A.) §51-7-1.
2. O.C.G.A. §51-7-2.
3. O.C.G.A. §35-2-32.
4. O.C.G.A. §35-2-33.
5. *Id.*
6. *Id.*
7. *Id.*
8. O.C.G.A. §35-3-4.

54 / ARREST

9. Blair v. State, 90 Ga. 326, 17 S.E. 96 (1892); Coker v. State, 14 Ga. App. 606, 81 S.E. 818 (1914).
10. *See* Cantrell v. Mayor & Council of Mt. Airy, 218 Ga. 646, 129 S.E. 2d 910 (1963); Shirley v. City of College Park, 102 Ga. App. 10, 115 S.E. 2d 469 (1960).
11. *See* O.C.G.A. §§6-30-20, 27.
12. Elder v. Camp, 193 Ga. 320, 322-23, 18 S.E. 2d 622, 625 (1942).
13. O.C.G.A. §17-4-25.
14. O.C.G.A. §36-8-5.
15. O.C.G.A. §§6-30-20, 27.
16. *See* Porter v. State, 124 Ga. 297, 299, 52 S.E. 283, 284 (1905).
17. O.C.G.A. §45-16-9.
18. O.C.G.A. §5A-350.
19. O.C.G.A. §42-5-35.
20. O.C.G.A. §27-1-18.
21. O.C.G.A. §42-8-38.
22. O.C.G.A. §§16-30-20 through -55.
23. O.C.G.A. §§16-13-70 through 76.
24. O.C.G.A. §26-4-51.
25. O.C.G.A. §25-2-9.
26. O.C.G.A. §35-2-71.
27. O.C.G.A. §50-16-6.
28. O.C.G.A. §37-1-21.
29. O.C.G.A. §20-3-72.

PART 2
SEARCH AND SEIZURE

9

Search and Seizure with a Warrant

The Fourth Amendment to the Constitution of the United States guarantees the right of the people to be secure against unreasonable searches and seizures. Because the protection of one's privacy against arbitrary intrusion by the police is at the core of the Fourth Amendment,[1] a search and seizure must be authorized by a search warrant. A warrantless search— without the special circumstances discussed in chapters 10 through 12—is unreasonable and therefore unlawful.[2] Requiring a warrant allows a neutral, detached magistrate to decide whether a search should be allowed.[3]

The United States Constitution gives only two requirements for the issuance of a search warrant. The first is that application for the warrant be made under oath or affirmation. The second is that the search warrant specify the places to be searched and describe with particularity the things to be seized. The procedure for obtaining and executing search warrants is left to the states to spell out by appropriate legislation. This chapter presents the procedure for obtaining and executing warrants in Georgia.

WHAT IS A SEARCH WARRANT?

A search warrant is a judicial command to "search the place or person particularly described in the warrant and to seize the instruments, articles, or things particularly described in the warrant."[4] It must be written, since Georgia law makes no provision for an oral or "telephone" warrant.[5] Figure 4 is a typical combination affidavit and search warrant.

58 / SEARCH AND SEIZURE

Figure 4. *Affidavit and Complaint for Search Warrant*

Georgia, Clarke County

CITY OF....., GEORGIA

Before... (Name and Title of Person before whom affidavit is made)...

The undersigned being duly sworn deposes and on oath says he has reason and probable cause to believe that certain property, namely .... is now being unlawfully concealed in and upon the premises known as .... located in the City of ...... Clarke County, Georgia, in the custody or control of .... and that deponent does verily believe and has probable cause to believe from facts within his knowledge as set out herein that the property heretofore described is kept and concealed in and upon said premises in violation of the laws of the State of Georgia and for the purpose of violating the same. The facts tending to establish affiant's reason for belief and probable cause for belief are as follows: ....

This affidavit and complaint is made for the purpose of authorizing the issuance of a search warrant for the person or premises described above.

Sworn to before me and subscribed in my presence this .... day of .... 19....

_____
Signature of Affiant

_____
Signature and Title of Officer before whom affidavit is made

GEORGIA, CLARKE COUNTY

To .... (Name of Peace Officer making complaint) .... and to all and singular the Peace Officers of the State of Georgia, "GREETING":

The foregoing affidavit and complaint having been duly made before me and the same, together with the facts submitted under oath contained therein having satisfied me that there is probable cause to believe that the property described therein is being unlawfully concealed in and upon the premises described therein of ....

YOU ARE HEREBY COMMANDED to enter and search said described premises, serving this warrant, and if the property described or any portion of it be found there to seize it, leaving a copy of this warrant and a receipt for the property taken, and prepare a written inventory of the property seized and return this warrant and bring the property before me within 10 days of this date or some other judicial officer, as required by law.

Given under my hand and seal this .... day of ...., 19.... at .... O'clock .... M.

_____
Signature and Title of Officer Issuing Search Warrant

RETURN

On . . . ., 19 . . . ., I executed the attached search warrant in the following manner:

1. Arrested . . . . and . . . .

2. Searched the person of the accused and the premises designated and other persons who were occupants of premises as follows: . . . .

3. Left a copy of the search warrant with . . . .

together with an inventory of the property taken in the search.

4. The property listed below was seized:. . . . .

. . . .

    I do solemnly swear that the property listed above is all the property seized by me on the search of the premises indicated in the attached warrant.

                                                                       EXECUTING OFFICER

Sworn and subscribed to before me
this the . . . . day of . . . ., 19 . . . .

          JUDGE

    Ten (10) days having expired from the date of issue of the attached warrant, the same is returned to the Judicial Officer who signed the same un-executed.

    This . . . . day of . . . ., 19 . . . .

                                                                               OFFICER

    The attached warrant not having been executed within ten (10) days and having been returned to the Court as un-executed, the same is hereby declared void.

    This . . . . day of . . . ., 19 . . . .

                                                               JUDICIAL OFFICER

Contents of a Search Warrant

To be valid a search warrant must contain the following information as required by the Georgia Code:*

1. the time and date of issuance [6]
2. the person who is to execute the warrant (generally its execution is directed to all peace officers of the state) [7]
3. a command to search the place or person particularly described in the warrant [8]
4. a command to seize the instruments, articles, or things particularly described in the warrant [9]

Particularity Requirement of a Search Warrant

The general rule regarding the particularity requirement (numbers 3 and 4 above) is that the descriptions found in the search warrant must be sufficient to allow a prudent officer executing it to be able to locate the person or place definitely and with reasonable certainty.[10] The requirement of particularity necessitates a description of the property to be seized that is accurate enough to identify it from all other property of the same kind.[11] The general test is whether the executing officer can determine exactly what can and cannot be seized based on descriptions in the warrant. A brief discussion below addresses what is and what is not sufficient regarding descriptions of places, automobiles, and persons.

Place. In describing premises to be searched, more care is generally required in urban than in rural areas. The authority to search the home of a named individual at a particular location includes authority to search the curtilage,[12] i.e., all the buildings in close proximity to the dwelling that are used in connection with it for family purposes,[13] such as a garage, storehouse, etc.

When the name of the owner or occupant is not given in a search warrant, the description of the premises must be exact.[14] For example, evidence seized at premises described by one street and number (293 South Rock Springs), under the authority of a search warrant directing a search of the premises of another street and number (283 Rock Springs), will not be allowed.[15] While the officers executing the search

---

*Note that Georgia Code or the Code is used as the abbreviated form of the Official Code of Georgia Annotated (O.C.G.A.).

warrant may know certain facts essential to the description of the premises, they may not supply these facts when they have been omitted from the warrant.[16] It is generally accepted that a subunit of multiunit premises may be identified by the name of the occupant.[17]

Automobiles. If the place to be searched is an automobile, a description specifically identifying that particular automobile is sufficient. Its location need not be given. A warrant describing the place to be searched as "a 1971 Ford, 4 dr. sdn., dark green over light green, bearing 1971 Georgia tag, Troup County No. LRK 645 in Houston County, Georgia," is a sufficient description of the "place," wherever it might be found.[18] However, a description that might fit several automobiles, rather than a particular one, would probably not be upheld. (See "Search of a Vehicle with a Warrant," p. 96, for a discussion of when a vehicle may be searched when it is on the curtilage of a residence for which a search warrant has been obtained.)

Person. Lack of specificity concerning a person to be searched may invalidate the search warrant. If a person's name is unknown, the search must be limited to a person of a specific physical description in a specific vicinity.[19] A warrant designating a person as "John Doe" would be valid where it names a white male, stocky build, black wavy hair, at a specific address in a specific apartment.[20] In contrast, a warrant authorizing the search of "John Doe," with no other description of the person, is invalid.[21] If a person is using a name as an alias, a search warrant describing the person by that name satisfies the particularity requirement.[22]

OBTAINING A SEARCH WARRANT

Who Can Get a Warrant?

"A search warrant may be issued only upon the application of an officer of the State or its political subdivisions charged with the duty of enforcing the criminal laws." A warrant may not be issued upon the application of a private citizen.[23]

Who Can Issue a Warrant?

The Fourth Amendment requires that search warrants be obtained from a neutral and detached judicial officer.[24] In Georgia, search warrants may be issued by any judicial officer authorized to hold a preliminary hearing.[25] This includes superior court judges, state court judges, magistrates, and justices of city or county courts.[26] All judicial officers may issue search warrants only in area(s) or county(ies) of their jurisdiction.[27] Warrants must be obtained from the judges directly and not merely from the court in which the judge is stationed.[28] Such warrants need not bear the seal of the court or the clerk of the court.[29] Since issuing a search warrant is a judicial act, this function may not be performed by nonjudicial officials such as court clerks.[30]

How Is a Warrant Obtained?

A person authorized to apply for a warrant may obtain one by submitting a written complaint under oath (affidavit) to a person authorized to issue warrants. (The previous page discusses who may get and who may issue a search warrant.) The affidavit must show probable cause that a crime is being, or has been committed, and it must particularly describe who or what is to be searched and what is to be seized.[31] The protection afforded by this procedure is that a disinterested and impartial magistrate, rather than a police officer or other person directly interested in conducting a search, determines whether the affidavit sets forth the necessary probable cause.[32] This procedure also ensures that the existence or nonexistence of probable cause will be judged before the search and uninfluenced by any evidence found as a result of the search.[33]

Thus, it is essential that the judicial officer actually determine probable cause. The judge's determination should be based on the facts stated in a written complaint or, in addition to the written complaint, on oral evidence taken under oath before the judge.[34] When a judicial officer fails to read the affidavit but merely attests to the affiant's signature, his or her subsequent issuance of a search warrant would be improper because a judicial determination of the existence of probable cause based on the facts contained in the affidavit would be lacking.[35]

Once the judicial official has determined probable cause, it is unnecessary that the affidavit supporting the search warrant be filed with the clerk of the court—or with the court if there is no clerk—until after execution of the warrant, or until the warrant has been returned "not executed."[36] However, it would be good policy for the police officer to suggest that the judge keep a copy of the affidavit.

CONTENTS OF AN AFFIDAVIT

An affidavit, like a search warrant, must meet certain statutory requirements. The Georgia Code requires that an affidavit

1. state facts sufficient to show probable cause (see below) that a crime is being, or has been committed, and
2. particularly describe the place or person, or both, to be searched and the things to be seized.[37]

The particularity requirements for an affidavit are the same as those for a search warrant. (Search warrant particularity requirements are discussed on p. 60.) Therefore, the requirement that the facts be sufficient to show probable cause is not satisfied by a mere statement of conclusion or belief on the part of the affiant; there must be details of "underlying circumstances" upon which the belief or conclusion is based.[38]

An affidavit may be based on hearsay information. It does not have to reflect the direct personal observations of the affiant, provided there are substantial grounds for believing the hearsay to be trustworthy.[39] However, for the issuance of a search warrant to be based on an informant's tip, the affidavit must

1. give reasons for the informant's reliability,
2. either state specifically how the informant obtained the information or describe the criminal activity in such detail that the magistrate may know it is more than a casual rumor or an accusation based merely on an individual's general reputation,[40] and
3. give a time period closely related to the approximate time of the commission of the offense within the affidavit to show that the information provided therein is not stale.[41]

While the informant need not be identified in the affidavit,[42] an anonymous tip or a rumor is not a sufficient basis for the issuance of a search warrant.[43] Observations of fellow officers also working on the federal or state government's investigation are a reliable basis for a search warrant applied for by one of them.[44]

Probable Cause

The probable cause required to be shown by the facts in the affidavit is more than mere suspicion, but the facts need not be enough to prove guilt beyond a reasonable doubt.[45] Considerably less is required to show probable cause for issuance of a search warrant than is required to prove guilt.[46] Basically, the facts must give a reasonable and prudent person, acting on the practical considerations of everyday life,[47] probable cause for believing that a crime has been committed or that evidence is being hidden on the premises specified in the affidavit. Courts and magistrates use a commonsense approach to test the facts contained in an affidavit; they attempt to avoid overly technical interpretations of search and seizure requirements.[48] As stated above, probable cause may be shown by hearsay information as long as there are sufficient facts to show that the information is true.

An important element that the magistrate must consider when making a determination of probable cause is the time the stated events occurred.[49] A finding of probable cause must be based on a showing of facts so closely related to the time of the search as to justify the conclusion that these facts still exist at the time the search warrant is issued.[50] For this reason, an affidavit in support of a search warrant must contain a statement of the time when the specified facts occurred. A judicial officer cannot independently determine whether probable cause still exists for the issuance of a search warrant when the application for such a warrant is supported solely by an affidavit that does not state the time of the occurrence in question.[51] An affidavit based on an informant's tip must state the time when the informant obtained the information, not the time when the information was relayed by the informant to the affiant.[52]

EXECUTING A SEARCH WARRANT

Who May Execute (Carry Out) a Search Warrant?

A judicial officer may direct a specific peace officer to execute a search warrant by naming that officer in the warrant. However, if the judicial officer fails to name a particular officer in the warrant, any peace officer in the state may execute it.[53] A law enforcement officer must execute any valid warrant placed in his or her hands,[54] and any refusal to do so constitutes an offense for which the officer may be indicted.[55]

Time of Execution

A warrant must be executed within 10 days of its issuance

or it becomes void and must be returned to the issuing officer as not executed.56 The Georgia Code does not state specifically what time of day the search warrant must be executed, only that it must be executed at a reasonable time.57 If the magistrate designates in the warrant the time of day it is to be executed, then the search warrant must be executed at that time. If a time of execution is not specified, the warrant may be executed at a reasonable time.

The courts have not yet defined the phrase a **reasonable time**. Therefore, the special facts and circumstances of each particular case will determine whether the warrant was executed at a reasonable time. It appears to be good policy to execute a warrant in the daytime unless there are good reasons for doing otherwise. In Georgia, a search warrant may be validly issued and executed on Sundays.58

Entering the Premises and the Use of Force

Before the officer executing a search warrant may enter the place to be searched, Georgia law requires that the officer give verbal notice of authority and the purpose for the entry to any persons on the premises.59 After giving such notice, or making a good-faith attempt to give such notice, the officer may use all necessary and reasonable force to gain entry if (1) entry is refused, (2) the place is unoccupied, or (3) the person or persons within the place refuse to acknowledge and answer the verbal notice.60

There are, however, some exceptions to the notice requirement. If the officer has reasonable grounds to believe that a warning would either greatly increase the officer's peril or lead to immediate destruction of evidence, the notice requirement will be excused.61 An excuse from notice is called a "no knock" provision and is contained in the warrant itself.62 Reasonable grounds for such belief may be supplied by an informant, whose identity need not be disclosed if his or her information meets the same tests as those for probable cause for the warrant issuance.63 For example, when an informant told the officer that one of the suspects had a pistol and had stated that he would not let the "fuzz" take him, and also that the suspects usually situated themselves near a sink or commode while cutting heroin so they could dispose of it quickly if the police came in, the court excused the notice requirement.64

While executing the search warrant, the officer may reasonably detain or search any person on the premises

1. to protect himself from attack, and
2. to prevent the disposal or concealment of anything particularly described in the warrant.65

However, an officer may not rely on O.C.G.A. 17-5-28(1) to search a person present on the premises who is not named in the warrant, to protect himself from attack, unless the officer has reasonable belief that the person is armed and dangerous. Where the officer "neither recognizes him as a person with a criminal history" or where the person "made no gestures or other actions indicative of an intent to commit an assault," the search of the unnamed person was improper.66 Merely to detain a person while conducting a lawful search is permissible even when the search uncovers illegal material and the detained person is subsequently arrested.67 Protection from attack and prevention of disposal or concealment of something described in the warrant are the only purposes for which the executing officer may search persons not identified in the warrant incident to a legitimate search of premises.68 Thus, where officers had no independent justification for searching a lady not named in the warrant, whom they knew to be a visitor from another state, the search of her purse was improper.69 This is the maximum extent to which the particularity of description required by the Fourth Amendment may be encroached upon by the realities of the situation.70 Even inserting the words "and any person present" in the warrant does not broaden the searching authorities' power to search persons not otherwise identified in the warrant beyond these limited terms.71 Naturally, the statute does not limit the officer's right to search persons when probable cause for a warrantless search exists.72

What May Be Seized?

Peace officers may seize any items particularly described in a search warrant. The Georgia Code provides that a warrant may be issued for the seizure of the following:73

1. any instrumentalities of the crime for which the warrant is issued
2. any person who has been kidnapped, or any human fetus or human corpse
3. stolen or embezzled property
4. any things which are unlawful to possess (contraband)
5. any tangible evidence of the crime for which the warrant is issued

A person's private papers may not be seized, with or without a warrant, if they are merely evidence of a crime,[74] but they may be seized if they are instrumentalities of a crime. For example, telephone numbers or betting tickets may be seized as instrumentalities of the crime of bookmaking.[75]

While carrying out a lawful search, an officer may seize any stolen or embezzled property, contraband, or other tangible evidence (other than a person's private papers) of the commission of a crime discovered regardless of whether the items seized were described in the warrant.[76] This is true even if the authorized search is not productive. In one case, while executing a warrant that authorized the seizure of counterfeit money and equipment the officers found some marijuana. Although the search never turned up the counterfeit money or equipment, the court found that the seizure of the marijuana was legal. The court stated that if in the course of an authorized search police officers find any contraband, they are authorized to seize it even though the items were not specified in the warrant.[77]

Limitations on the Search

One restriction on the scope of the search is that officers executing a search warrant are limited to actions necessary in searching for items listed in the warrant. These "necessary actions" will vary according to the nature of the evidence sought. Thus, when executing a search warrant that authorized the seizure of equipment and records used in an illegal wagering business, officers could search through desk drawers.[78] It reasonably follows that while executing a warrant which directs a search for a moonshine still, an officer may not search through desk drawers. Thus, officers are limited to actions necessary to locate the items listed in the warrant. Once the items are located the search must be discontinued.

For the legal seizure of contraband evidence not specified in the warrant, such matter must come into the plain view (see next chapter) of the officer while making a lawful search.[79] That is, while searching for items specified in the warrant and while staying within the scope of the search, the officer may seize evidence of other crimes (contraband).

Requirement to Leave a Copy of the Warrant

If a warrant is executed, the officer is required to leave a duplicate copy of the warrant with any person from whom any articles were seized. If no one is present, the officer must leave the copy in a conspicuous place on the premises.[80]

Return to Court of Warrant, Items Seized, and Inventory

A written return of the warrant and the articles seized must be made without unnecessary delay to the judicial officer who issued the warrant or to any court of competent jurisdiction.[81] An inventory of the articles seized, signed under oath by the officer who conducted the search, must be filed with the return.[82] The inventory must be completed in an original with two copies.[83] The items mentioned in the inventory should be described with the same detail as in the application for the warrant. Upon request, the judicial officer issuing the warrant must deliver a copy of the inventory list to the applicant and to the person from whom the articles were taken.[84] Of course, if the arrestee is later released without a charge, all articles seized (other than illegal contraband) must be returned to him or her.

ENDNOTES

1. Berger v. New York, 388 U.S. 41, 53 (1967); Wolf v. Colorado, 338 U.S. 25, 27-28 (1949).
2. Coolidge v. New Hampshire, 403 U.S. 443 (1971); Chimel v. California, 395 U.S. 752 (1969).
3. Coolidge v. New Hampshire, 403 U.S. 443 (1971).
4. OFFICIAL CODE OF GA. ANN. (O.C.G.A.) §17-5-23.
5. Walker v. State, 220 Ga. 415, 419-20, 139 S.E. 2d, 278, 282 (1964) reversed; on other grounds 381 U.S. 355 (1965).
6. O.C.G.A. §17-5-22.
7. O.C.G.A. §17-5-24.
8. O.C.G.A. §17-5-23.
9. *Id.*
10. Buck v. State, 127 Ga. App. 72, 73, 192 S.E. 2d 432 (1972); Steele v. United States, 267 U.S. 498, 503 (1925).
11. Marron v. United States, 275 U.S. 192 (1927).
12. Moon v. State, 120 Ga. App. 141, 169 S.E. 2d 632-36 (1969).
13. Wright v. State, 12 Ga. App. 514, 77 S.E. 657 (1913).
14. Garner v. State, 124 Ga. App. 33, 35, 182 S.E. 2d 902, 904 (1971).
15. Bell v. State, 124 Ga. App. 139, 182 S.E. 2d 901 (1971).
16. Bell v. State, *supra* note 15 at 140.
17. Garner v. State, 124 Ga. App. 33, 35, 182 S.E. 2d 902, 904-5 (1971).
18. Reed v. State, 126 Ga. App. 323, 190 S.E. 2d 587 (1972).
19. Fomby v. State, 120 Ga. App. 387, 170 S.E. 2d 585, 586 (1969).
20. United States v. Ferrone, 438 F. 2d 381 (3rd Cir. 1971); Fomby v. State, *supra* note 19.
21. Fowler v. State, 128 Ga. App. 501, 502, 197 S.E. 2d 502, 503 (1973).
22. Thrall v. State, 122 Ga. App. 427, 177 S.E. 2d 192 (1970).

23. O.C.G.A. §17-5-20.
24. Coolidge v. New Hampshire, 403 U.S. 443 (1971).
25. O.C.G.A. §17-5-21.
26. O.C.G.A. §17-7-20.
27. O.C.G.A. §17-5-22.
28. *Id.*
29. O.C.G.A. §17-5-22(a).
30. Cox v. Perkins, 151 Ga. 632, 107 S.E. 863 (1921).
31. O.C.G.A. §17-5-21.
32. Giordenello v. United States, 357 U.S. 480, 486 (1958); Patterson v. State, 126 Ga. App. 753, 191 S.E. 2d 584 (1972).
33. Dresch v. State, 125 Ga. App. 110, 186 S.E. 2d 496, 498 (1971).
34. Campbell v. State, 226 Ga. 883, 178 S.E. 2d 257 (1970).
35. Reid v. State, 129 Ga. App. 660, 200 S.E. 2d 456 (1973).
36. O.C.G.A. §17-5-22.
37. O.C.G.A. §17-5-21.
38. United States v. Ventresca, 380 U.S. 102, 108 (1965).
39. Jones v. United States, 362 U.S. 257 (1960); Carson v. State, 221 Ga. 299, 144 S.E. 2d 384 (1965); Reece v. State, 152 Ga. App. 760, 264 S.E. 2d 258 (1979).
40. Spinelli v. United States, 393 U.S. 410 (1969); Aguilar v. Texas, 378 U.S. 108 (1964); Carson v. State, 221 Ga. 299, 144 S.E. 2d 384 (1965); Buck v. State, 127 Ga. App. 72, 192 S.E. 2d 432 (1972); Sams v. State, 121 Ga. App. 46, 172 S.E. 2d 473 (1970).
41. State v. Watts, 154 Ga. App. 789, 270 S.E. 2d 52 (1980).
42. Rugendorf v. United States, 376 U.S. 528 (1964); Buck v. State, *supra* note 40; Register v. State, 124 Ga. App. 136, 183 S.E. 2d 68 (1971).
43. Thornton v. State, 125 Ga. App. 374, 187 S.E. 2d 583 (1972).
44. United States v. Ventresca, 380 U.S. 102 (1965); Buck v. State, 127 Ga. App. 72, 74, 192 S.E. 2d 432, 434 (1972).
45. United States v. Harris, 403 U.S. 573 (1971).
46. Draper v. United States, 358 U.S. 307 (1959); Geiger v. State, 129 Ga. App. 488, 492, 199 S.E. 2d 861, 864 (1973).
47. Strauss v. Stynchcombe, 224 Ga. 859, 165 S.E. 2d 302, 306 (1968).
48. United States v. Ventresca, 380 U.S. 102, 108-9 (1965).
49. Fowler v. State, 121 Ga. App. 22, 172 S.E. 2d 447 (1970).
50. Sgro v. United States, 287 U.S. 206 (1932); Wood v. State, 118 Ga. App. 477, 164 S.E. 2d 233 (1968).
51. Fowler v. State, *supra* note 49.
52. Windsor v. State, 122 Ga. App. 767, 178 S.E. 2d 751 (1970).
53. O.C.G.A. §17-5-24.
54. O.C.G.A. §17-4-24.
55. Newkirk v. State, 57 Ga. App. 803, 807, 196 S.E. 911, 913 (1938); Ormand v. Ball, 120 Ga. 916, 48 S.E. 383 (1904).
56. O.C.G.A. §17-5-25.
57. O.C.G.A. §17-5-26.
58. Veasey v. State, 113 Ga. App. 187, 147 S.E. 2d 515 (1966).

59. O.C.G.A. §17-5-27.
60. *Id.*
61. Jones v. State, 127 Ga. App. 137, 193 S.E. 2d 38, 39 (1972); Scull v. State, 122 Ga. App. 696, 178 S.E. 2d 270 (1970).
62. Jones v. State, 127 Ga. App. 137, 193 S.E. 2d 38 (1972).
63. Scull v. State, *supra* note 61.
64. *Id.*
65. O.C.G.A. §17-5-28; Michigan v. Summers, 452 U.S. 692 (1980).
66. Bundy v. State, 168 Ga. App. 90, 91, 308 S.E. 2d 213, 215 (1983), citing Ybarra v. Illinois, 444 U.S. 85, 93 (1979).
67. Michigan v. Summers, 452 U.S. 692 (1980).
68. Wallace v. State, 131 Ga. App. 204, 205 S.E. 2d 523 (1974); Michigan v. Summers, 452 U.S. 692 (1980).
69. Hawkins v. State, 165 Ga. App. 278, 300 S.E. 2d 224 (1983).
70. *Id.*
71. *Id.*
72. *Id.*
73. O.C.G.A. §17-5-21(a).
74. O.C.G.A. §17-5-21(a)(5).
75. O.C.G.A. §17-5-21(a)(1).
76. O.C.G.A. §17-5-21(a)(5).
77. Bostwick v. State, 124 Ga. App. 113, 182 S.E. 2d 925 (1971).
78. Stanley v. State, 224 Ga. 259, 161 S.E. 2d 309 (1968).
79. Stanley v. Georgia, 394 U.S. 557, 571 (1969). (concurring opinion)
80. O.C.G.A. §17-5-25.
81. O.C.G.A. §17-5-29.
82. *Id.*
83. *Id.*
84. O.C.G.A. §17-8-29.

10

Exceptions to the Search Warrant Requirement

Although there is a definite constitutional preference for searches to be made under the authority of a search warrant,[1] the overwhelming majority are made without a warrant. As previously discussed, the general rule is that the search of private property without a warrant is unreasonable, and thus unlawful.[2] However, in certain carefully defined cases a warrantless search is reasonable.[3] The exceptions to the warrant requirement serve the legitimate needs of law enforcement officers to protect their own well-being and to preserve evidence from destruction.[4]

This chapter focuses on the general exceptions to the search warrant requirement, i.e., consent searches, plain view searches, searches under circumstances requiring immediate action, and searches incident to a lawful arrest. The following three chapters concern the more specific problems of how and when the general exceptions apply to permit a warrantless search of premises (Chapter 11), a person (Chapter 12), or of a vehicle (Chapter 13).

SEARCH AND SEIZURE BY CONSENT

Like other constitutional safeguards, the right to be secure against unreasonable searches and seizures may be waived.[5] Thus, a "search" to which an individual voluntarily consents satisfies Fourth Amendment requirements[6] and is not illegal.[7] Consent may be oral or written. It may be implied from the acts or conduct of the defendant; for instance, when the defendant does not object to the search and cooperates by opening the trunk of his or her car.[8]

Consent must be voluntary and it must be given in complete absence of actual or implied duress or coercion. For example, a search is invalid if the "consent" is given only after the police official conducting it asserted possession of a search warrant, when in fact there was none.[9] Essentially, how voluntary the consent was will be determined from circumstances surrounding each case. The courts will consider the suspect's knowledge of his or her right to refuse, as well as age, education, race, and similar facts.[10]

The question of who other than the suspect may give consent is also a factor in the validity of a consent search. A landlord may not consent to the search of rented premises occupied by a tenant,[11] nor may a hotel clerk consent to a search of a guest's room.[12] But a spouse may consent to a search of premises she or he jointly occupies with the other spouse.[13] And a father may consent to the search of his minor son's automobile parked on the father's property.[14] The cases indicate that if a person other than the suspect has a possessory interest in the place to be searched, and consents, it is sufficient to authorize the search.[15]

PLAIN VIEW

Under the **plain view doctrine**, mere observation by an officer does not constitute a search and, consequently, the principles of the law of search and seizure are not applicable. Since a search is a prying quest for something hidden from observation, no search is made merely by looking at what is not concealed. The courts have held that there is no search when the items in question are voluntarily exhibited to police officers,[16] and that an officer is free to seize what is in plain sight.[17]

However, there are some limits to the applicability of the plain view doctrine.

1. The officer must have had a right to be at the place from which the items were viewed.[18] For example, if the officer were trespassing on the defendant's property, a plain view seizure would not be valid. But if an officer were conducting a valid license check and observed burglary tools and stolen goods on the floor of an automobile, the items would be held to have been in plain view.[19]

2. No action on the part of the officer may be taken to bring the items into plain view (or it would probably be a

search). But using artificial lighting, such as a flashlight, to bring the article into plain view does not constitute a search.[20]

3. The incriminating nature of the seized object must be apparent from its appearance. For example: An officer stopped a defendant for speeding and subsequently saw a bag between the brakes and the steering wheel. He could not see the contents of the bag (marijuana). The seizure of the bag was ruled illegal because it was not immediately apparent to the officer that incriminating evidence was before him.[21] However, in a case where the officer could see into a grocery bag on the floor of the car's rear seat and identify a substance as marijuana, the seizure was allowed.[22] An officer cannot unwrap a package or make a preliminary exploration to determine whether an object is illegal without a search warrant.

4. Under the plain view doctrine, the discovery of evidence must be inadvertent or accidental. The planned search may not extend to the seizure of objects that the officers know in advance will be found in plain view and that they intend to seize.[23] This rule applies to contraband and stolen property as well as other tangible evidence. So if law enforcement officers anticipate that they will find incriminating evidence in a particular place before entering, and if there is no substantial danger that taking the time to obtain a valid warrant will result in the disappearance of evidence, the officers must obtain a valid warrant authorizing the seizure of such evidence.

It is important to note that the plain view doctrine is used in three distinct situations:

1. during observation not amounting to a search
2. within the scope of a search under a warrant[24] (because the officer has a right to be where he or she is when executing a warrant)
3. when there is a seizure of items discovered in a warrantless search[25]

SEARCH AND SEIZURE UNDER EXIGENT CIRCUMSTANCES

Warrantless searches can be made in situations where officers have probable cause for the search and **exigent circumstances** (i.e., those requiring immediate action) make it impractical to obtain a warrant.[26] As a rule, exigent circumstances are those in which a suspect is fleeing or instrumentalities of a crime are in the process of being destroyed.[27]

The first requirement for this exception is that the officer conducting the search must have probable cause to believe that an instrumentality or evidence of a crime will be found.[28] Generally, **probable cause** exists when the facts and circumstances of which the officer has reasonably reliable information are sufficient to justify the belief that an offense has been or is being committed.[29]

Since probable cause alone cannot justify a warrantless seizure, the second requirement is that there must also be exigent circumstances under which it is not practical to obtain a warrant.[30] In the situation where officers were informed that an armed robbery had taken place and that a suspect who was observed fleeing the scene had entered a particular house, the court held that the exigencies of the situation made it imperative that they enter the house without a warrant and search for the suspect and the weapons used by him in the robbery.[31] Likewise, the warrantless search of the defendant's car trunk for a gun, where the car was vulnerable to intrusion by vandals, was ruled proper.[32]

However, mere inconvenience in obtaining a warrant or slight delay in the preparation of papers and presentation of evidence to a magistrate will not support a warrantless search under this exception.[33] The exigencies of the situation must make search without a warrant imperative.[34] Consequently, the warrantless search and seizure of a still in an unoccupied house was not justified since there was no urgency for making a prompt search.[35]

When there is probable cause to search, exigent circumstances often exist to justify the warrantless search of an automobile, because the car is movable[36] (See p. 88, "Stopping and Searching Moving Vehicles Suspected of Carrying Contraband.") Excluding autos, most of the searches conducted under this exception are those made when police enter premises without a warrant in "hot pursuit" of an offender.[37] (See "Hot Pursuit," p. 79, for further discussion.)

SEARCH INCIDENT TO A LAWFUL ARREST

One of the well-established exceptions to the general rule requiring search warrants is the search incident to a lawful arrest.[38] The policy behind this exception is that without such a search, the officer's safety might be endangered and the arrest frustrated. In addition, evidence on the person of the arrested party could be concealed or destroyed. For such a search to be valid, the arrest must be lawful. If the arrest is lawful, the search is legal; but if the arrest is not lawful, the search is illegal.[39]

Lawful arrests fall into two categories: those made with a warrant and those made without a warrant. For an arrest with a warrant to be valid, (a) there must be probable cause to believe that the suspect has committed a crime and (b) procedural requirements must be complied with in procuring the arrest warrant. An officer may make a lawful arrest without a warrant if an offense is committed in his presence, when an offender is trying to escape, or when a failure of justice is likely for lack of an official to issue a warrant.[40] (See Part I, Chapter 2, "Arrest with a Warrant," and Chapter 3, "Arrest without a Warrant.")

Once a person has been lawfully arrested, the person is under the control of the arresting officer. With any freedom of movement permitted an arrestee by the officer, such as a brief stop at the arrestee's home or automobile to obtain identification, the officer may accompany the arrestee without the necessity of a search warrant or the existence of exigent circumstances. (See discussion of "Search and Seizure under Exigent Circumstances," p. 73.) The officer may stay close to the arrestee at all times, literally at his or her elbow, because every arrestee must be presumed to present a risk of harm to the officer. Therefore, any liberty allowed the arrestee by the officer is considered consent by the arrestee for the officer to accompany the arrestee. The officer cannot be considered as trespassing, and any items discovered by merely looking around under these circumstances fall within the plain view doctrine.[41]

In addition to the lawful arrest requirement, either with or without a warrant, there are other limitations on a search incident to an arrest. The search must be **substantially contemporaneous** or, in other words, take place at approximately the same time the arrest does. Usually the search follows the arrest, but in certain cases the search may slightly precede the formal arrest.[42] Even in these cases, probable cause for the arrest must exist before the search is made. It cannot be furnished by products of the search. Searches and seizures that could be made on the spot at the time and place of arrest may be made later at the place of detention.[43] The important point is that the search may not be used to provide the basis for the arrest.[44]

The scope of a warrantless search incident to arrest is

limited to the area within the defendant's immediate control or reach.[45] The arresting officer may search this area to

1. protect himself from attack,
2. prevent the arrested person from escaping,
3. discover and seize the fruits of the crime for which the suspect was arrested, and
4. discover and seize instruments, articles, or things which are being used or which may have been used in the commission of the crime for which the person has been arrested.[46]

This section has examined the general requirements and limitations of a warrantless search incident to an arrest. More specific limitation of warrantless searches of premises, persons, and automobiles incident to arrest will be discussed in the next three chapters.

ENDNOTES

1. United States v. Ventresca, 380 U.S. 102, 105-6 (1965).
2. Chimel v. California, 395 U.S. 752 (1969); Katz v. United States, 389 U.S. 347 (1967).
3. Id.
4. United States v. United States Dist. Ct., 407 U.S. 297 (1972).
5. Zap v. United States, 328 U.S. 624 (1946).
6. Katz v. United States, 389 U.S. 347 (1967).
7. Hightower v. State, 228 Ga. 301, 185 S.E. 2d 82 (1971).
8. Young v. State, 113 Ga. App. 497, 148 S.E. 2d 461 (1966).
9. Bumper v. North Carolina, 391 U.S. 543 (1968).
10. Schneckloth v. Bustamonte, 412 U.S. 218 (1973).
11. Chapman v. United States, 365 U.S. 610 (1961).
12. Stoner v. California, 376 U.S. 483 (1964).
13. Coolidge v. New Hampshire, 403 U.S. 443 (1971); Messer v. State, 120 Ga. App. 747, 172 S.E. 2d 194 (1969); cert. denied, 400 U.S. 866 (1970).
14. Tolbert v. State, 224 Ga. 291, 161 S.E. 2d 279 (1968).
15. Braddock v. State, 127 Ga. App. 513, 517-18, 194 S.E. 2d 317, 320 (1972); Garrison v. State, 122 Ga. App. 757, 758, 178 S.E. 2d 744, 746 (1970); Montgomery v. State, 155 Ga. App. 423, 270 S.E. 2d 825 (1980).
16. Katz v. United States, 389 U.S. 347, 351 (1967); Lewis v. United States, 385 U.S. 206, 210 (1966); United States v. Lee, 274 U.S. 559, 563 (1927).
17. Harris v. United States, 390 U.S. 234, 236 (1968); Ker v. California, 374 U.S. 23 (1963); Brewer v. State, 129 Ga. App. 118, 199 S.E. 2d 109 (1973).
18. Id.
19. Anderson v. State, 123 Ga. App. 57, 179 S.E. 2d 286 (1970).
20. United States v. Lee, 274 U.S. 559 (1927); Caito v. State, 130 Ga. App. 831, 204 S.E. 2d 765 (1974).

21. Mobley v. State, 130 Ga. App. 80, 202 S.E. 2d 465 (1973).
22. Williams v. State, 129 Ga. App. 103, 198 S.E. 2d 683 (1973).
23. Coolidge v. New Hampshire, 403 U.S. 443 (1971).
24. OFFICIAL CODE OF GA. ANN. (O.C.G.A.) §17-5-1(a)(5).
25. O.C.G.A. §17-5-1(a)(4).
26. Coolidge v. New Hampshire, 403 U.S. 443 (1971); Chambers v. Maroney, 399 U.S. 42 (1970); Warden v. Hayden, 387 U.S. 294 (1967).
27. McDonald v. United States, 335 U.S. 451, 455 (1948).
28. Dyke v. Taylor Impl. Mfg. Co., 391 U.S. 216 (1968).
29. Berger v. New York, 388 U.S. 41, 55 (1967); Brinegar v. United States, 338 U.S. 160, 175-76 (1949); Carroll v. United States, 267 U.S. 132, 149 (1925). *See also* discussion of probable cause and informant's tips on pp. 10-12.
30. Coolidge v. New Hampshire, 403 U.S. 443 (1971); Warden v. Hayden, 387 U.S. 294 (1967).
31. Warden v. Hayden, 387 U.S. 294 (1967).
32. Cady v. Dombrowski, 413 U.S. 433 (1973).
33. McDonald v. United States, 335 U.S. 451, 455 (1948); Zap v. United States, *supra* note 5.
34. McDonald v. United States, 335 U.S. 454-55 (1948).
35. Chapman v. United States, 365 U.S. 610 (1961).
36. Carroll v. United States, 267 U.S. 132 (1925).
37. Warden v. Hayden, 387 U.S. 294 (1967).
38. O.C.G.A. §17-5-1.
39. Kelly v. State, 129 Ga. App. 131, 198 S.E. 2d 910 (1973); Bethea v. State, 127 Ga. App. 97, 192 S.E. 2d 554 (1972).
40. O.C.G.A. §17-4-20.
41. Washington v. Chrisman, 454 U.S. 1 (1981).
42. Cupp v. Murphy, 412 U.S. 291 (1973); Ker v. California, 374 U.S. 23, 42-43 (1963).
43. United States v. Edwards, 415 U.S. 800, (1974).
44. Kelley v. State, 129 Ga. App. 131, 198 S.E. 2d 910 (1973); Bethea v. State, 127 Ga. App. 97, 192 S.E. 2d 554 (1972).
45. O.C.G.A. §17-5-1.
46. *Id.*

Search of Premises without a Warrant

General exceptions to the search warrant requirement were discussed in the previous chapter. This chapter cites the exceptions that allow warrantless searches of premises. The consent and plain view exceptions discussed on pages 71 and 72 are applicable to searches of premises. Because the Fourth Amendment imposes greater limitations on the search of premises, warrantless searches incident to lawful arrests and those under the exigent circumstance of hot pursuit are further explained.

SEARCH OF PREMISES INCIDENT TO A LAWFUL ARREST

For the general requirements of a search incident to a lawful arrest, see "Search Incident to a Lawful Arrest," page 74. A search of premises incident to an arrest generally can be made only if the arrest took place there.[1] If an arrest is made two blocks away from the defendant's apartment, search of the apartment would not be "substantially contemporaneous with the arrest,"[2] and it would not fall under this exception. Likewise, a search of the defendant's hotel room cannot be held incident to the defendant's arrest on the street, even though in close proximity to the hotel entrance.

Even if the arrest takes place on the premises, it does not authorize the arresting officer to make an unlimited search of the premises. The Georgia Code limits such a search to the area within the arrested person's immediate presence.[3] Also, as with searches incident to a lawful arrest (see p. 74), the search may be only for the purposes of

1. self-protection of the officer from attack,
2. preventing the arrested person from escaping,

3. discovering and seizing the fruits of the crime for which the person has been arrested, and
4. discovering and seizing any instruments, articles, or things which are being used or which have been used in the commission of the crime for which the person has been arrested.[4]

For example, if a person were arrested in the kitchen, a search of the bedroom could not be justified as incident to a lawful arrest because the bedroom would be an area outside the arrestee's immediate control. If a person were arrested on a rape charge, and after the arrest the officer were in no danger of attack and there were no chance of the arrestee's escape, a search of the area in his or her immediate presence would not be lawful because it would not fall under the four valid purposes listed above.

For a search of premises incident to an arrest to be valid, three requirements must be met:

1. the arrest must have taken place on the premises,
2. the search may not extend past the arrested person's immediate presence, and
3. the search must have been for one of the four authorized purposes.

A general rule of thumb for determining the space within the suspect's immediate presence or control is an arm-length span around the suspect. This is a reasonable distance in which the suspect may have concealed weapons or fruits and instrumentalities of a crime.[5]

HOT PURSUIT

While in hot pursuit of a fleeing suspected felon, the pursuing officers may enter a house in which they have probable cause to believe the suspect is hiding and they may search for the suspect or any weapons that he or she might use.[6] The permissible scope of the search may be as broad as is reasonably necessary to prevent the danger that the suspect may resist or escape.[7] The reason for this exception is that the Fourth Amendment does not require police officers to delay an investigation if doing so would gravely endanger their lives or the lives of others.[8]

Actually, the search of premises without a warrant while in hot pursuit of a fleeing suspected felon combines the exigent circumstances exception and the plain view doctrine. (See p. 72, "Plain View"; p. 73, "Search and Seizure under Exigent Circumstances.") As discussed previously, a police officer is free to use and seize objects in plain sight if he or she has a right to be at that particular place.[9] Since the exigency of the hot pursuit situation gives the officer the right to be in the house to search for the suspect or his weapons,[10] the officer may seize anything that comes into plain view while conducting such a search.

ENDNOTES

1. Shipley v. California, 395 U.S. 818, 820 (1969); James v. Louisiana, 382 U.S. 36, 37 (1965).
2. James v. Louisiana, 382 U.S. 36 (1965).
3. OFFICIAL CODE OF GA. ANN. (O.C.G.A.) §17-5-1.
4. *Id.*
5. Chimel v. California, 395 U.S. 752 (1969).
6. Warden v. Hayden, 387 U.S. 294 (1967).
7. *Id.*
8. *Id.*
9. Ker v. California, 374 U.S. 23 (1963); Brooks v. State, 129 Ga. App. 393, 199 S.E. 2d 578 (1973).
10. Warden v. Hayden, 387 U.S. 294 (1967).

12

Search of the Person without a Warrant

Some unique problems are encountered when the general exceptions to the search warrant requirement, discussed previously in Chapter 10, are applied to warrantless searches of the person. As with warrantless searches of premises, the consent and plain view exceptions are essentially the same and need no further discussion. The stop and frisk search, recent developments in the search of a person or persons incident to arrest, and the search of the body itself will be discussed in this chapter.

One of the primary problems in the law of search and seizure is the question of which passengers may be searched when a vehicle is stopped by law enforcement officers. Although this technically is a search of the person, it is primarily a search of vehicle problem. For a discussion of vehicle searches, see Chapter 13.

STOP AND FRISK

The **stop and frisk** exception is the procedure in which an officer may make an on-the-street stop, interrogation, and pat-down for weapons. A stop and frisk is actually a two-step process, and a reasonable suspicion that the suspect is engaging in criminal conduct is necessary both for the stop and for the frisk.[1] The **stop**, the first step of a stop and frisk, allows an officer to stop a suspect if the officer has reasonable suspicion, based on natural senses, experience, and good judgment, that criminal activity might be afoot.[2] Such a stop may be made when there is insufficient probable cause for either arrest or a warrantless search.[3] The officer may base the stop on a tip from an informant.[4] After identifying him- or herself, the officer may ask the suspect's name, address, reason for presence, and other similar questions.

After making the stop, the officer may, on the basis of a reasonable suspicion that the suspect is armed and dangerous, frisk the person.[5] The **frisk**, the second step of the stop and frisk, is actually a search limited to a pat-down of the suspect's outer clothing for a gun or other weapon. It assures the officer that the suspect is not going to turn on the officer with a weapon.[6] An officer who discovers a weapon during the frisk may seize it, arrest the suspect, and proceed with further investigation. The sole justification for this warrantless intrusion is the protection of the officer and others nearby. A thorough search of the suspect can never be justified by calling it a frisk.[7]

Precise limitations upon this protective search and seizure are not easily formulated and must be developed on a case-by-case basis.[8] A stop and frisk was justified when an officer concluded that a robbery was planned after observing two men hovering about a street corner for an extended period, pacing along an identical route, and pausing to stare in the same store window 24 times.[9] In another case, when a suspect matched the description of a wanted man and a bulge was observed under his shirt, law enforcement officers could validly stop and frisk the suspect.[10] The basic guidelines for a stop and frisk are as follows:

1. An officer may stop and momentarily detain a suspect for questioning if the circumstances indicate that criminal activity is afoot.
2. The officer may conduct a pat-down of the suspect's outer clothing (frisk) if, after the stop, the officer has a reasonable suspicion that the suspect is armed and dangerous.[11]

SEARCH OF PERSON INCIDENT TO A LAWFUL ARREST

The general requirements and limitations of a warrantless search incident to an arrest were discussed in Chapter 10, "Search Incident to a Lawful Arrest," p. 74. However, a warrantless search of the person incident to a lawful arrest differs from a warrantless search of either premises or an automobile incident to arrest. A Supreme Court decision broadened the permissible scope of a warrantless search incident to an arrest to permit a police officer to make a full body search of a person who is under custodial arrest.[12]

As with any search incident to an arrest, the arrest must be lawful before the search can be legal.[13] The search may not precede the arrest nor may it serve as justification for the arrest itself.[14] For example, a search incident to an arrest was held illegal when the arresting officer lacked probable cause to arrest the suspect at that time even though the search subsequently revealed marijuana.[15]

Once the suspect has been placed under lawful custodial arrest, the officer may make a full search of his or her person regardless of whether or not the officer fears the suspect to be armed.[16] It is important to note that only a full arrest, with a taking into custody, can support a search incident to a lawful arrest. Thus, the situation in which an errant motorist is merely issued a citation directing a court appearance at a later date will not support a warrantless search.

It is not necessary for the search to be made at the same time and place as the arrest. It may be conducted later when the accused has been taken to a place of detention.[17]

SEARCH OF THE BODY

Extractions of body fluids, such as blood, or other penetrations into the body are also protected against by the Fourth Amendment. However, a warrantless search of this type can be made in exigent circumstances. Extraction of a blood sample by a hospital physician at the instruction of police was lawful when the officers had probable cause to believe the suspect was guilty of drunken driving.[18] Because the incriminating evidence (the alcohol content of the blood) would have disappeared before a search warrant could have been obtained, the officers were justified in proceeding without one. Since this exception has not been extended, it is advisable, as a matter of procedure, for peace officers to detain the suspect and obtain a warrant.

It should be noted that even though a search of the body might otherwise be valid, it can be made unlawful by the manner in which it is conducted. These searches are often struck down because they involve a forcible and revolting procedure in violation of the general due process requirement of the Fifth Amendment. Examples of invalidated searches include use of a stomach pump[19] and the forcible administration of emetics or laxatives.[20]

Georgia has an **implied consent** statute which provides that a police officer may request a breath test incident to a lawful arrest of a person whom the officer has reasonable cause to believe is driving under the influence of alcohol.[21] A blood test may also be given, under carefully regulated conditions,[22] with the suspect's consent. If the suspect refuses any test, administrative proceedings will be instituted to suspend his or her driver's license.[23] But this statute does not, under any circumstances, authorize the forceful administration of the breathalizer test.

SEARCHES AS PART OF POLICE PROCEDURE

There is a distinction between what actions may be taken (a) by an officer making a search incident to an arrest and (b) by custodial officers at the "booking in" process prior to incarcerating the prisoner. As noted on p. 74, under a search incident to an arrest, the search ordinarily must be conducted at the time and place of arrest. A custodial search occurs at a different time and place, such as when the prisoner's property is taken for safekeeping while the prisoner is in jail. Inventory searches are generally justified as being necessary to protect the owner's property and to safeguard the police from false claims for lost possessions.[24] Evidence obtained as a result of a routine inventory conducted to itemize the property of an arrested person is admissible.[25]

Abuse of the inventory search has led to court limitations on the use of evidence found during the inventory process. For example, once an inventory has been accomplished, officers do not have an unlimited right to reinspect the arrestee's property without first obtaining a search warrant.[26]

Since fingerprinting constitutes a search of the person, it is subject to the proscriptions of the Fourth Amendment against unreasonable searches and seizures.[27] Like the inventory search of the person following an arrest, fingerprinting is generally considered to be part of the booking process. Fingerprints taken after a valid arrest are generally upheld as reasonable[28] and are admissible as evidence.[29] It is also permissible to take the fingerprints of a suspect during the investigatory process even if an actual arrest has not been made. In such a case, of course, there must be sufficient probable cause to believe that the suspect has committed a crime.[30] Fingerprints taken of persons when there was no probable cause to suspect them of a crime are inadmissible.[31]

It should be noted, in reference to "a search of a person incident to a lawful arrest" or "a search of the body," that these searches include "strip searches," when such are conducted for the purposes of and within the boundaries established in the Georgia Code (see first paragraph of this section). However, once a person is under arrest and is incarcerated, he or she becomes a pretrial detainee, not yet convicted of a crime, who is awaiting trial or pretrial release. In Bell v. Wolfish,[32] the Supreme Court held that such pretrial detainees retain some Fourth Amendment protections and stated that once a person is incarcerated as a pretrial detainee, a strip search of such a person can be constitutional only if the search is reasonable in light of the circumstances surrounding the search. There must be a balancing of the detainee's personal rights and the state's need to invade them.[33]

Once the close relationship of the initial arrest and any searches necessitated by that arrest has passed into a routine holding of a pretrial detainee, the Code boundaries and restrictions no longer apply. Any searches, strip or otherwise, conducted as part of the holding process should be done only with regard to the Supreme Court's holding in Bell.[34]

ENDNOTES

1. Terry v. Ohio, 392 U.S. 1, 24, 26-27 (1968); Jones v. State, 126 Ga. App. 841, 843, 192 S.E. 2d 171, 173 (1972).
2. Terry v. Ohio, 392 U.S. 1 (1968).
3. Brooks v. State, 129 Ga. App. 109, 111, 198 S.E. 2d 892, 894 (1973).
4. Adams v. Williams, 407 U.S. 143 (1972).
5. Terry v. Ohio, 392 U.S. 1 (1968).
6. L.B.B. v. State, 129 Ga. App. 163, 198 S.E. 2d 895, 896 (1973).
7. *Id.* at 895; Holtzendorf v. State, 125 Ga. App. 747-50, 188 S.E. 2d 879, 881 (1972).
8. Terry v. Ohio, 392 U.S. 1, 22 (1968).
9. Terry v. Ohio, 392 U.S. 1, 24, 26-27 (1968).
10. Alexander v. State, 225 Ga. 358, 360, 168 S.E. 2d 315, 317 (1969).
11. Terry v. Ohio, 392 U.S. 1 (1968).
12. United States v. Robinson, 414 U.S. 218 (1973).
13. Bethea v. State, 127 Ga. App. 97, 192 S.E. 2d 554 (1972).
14. Kelley v. State, 129 Ga. App. 131, 198 S.E. 2d 910 (1973).
15. *Id.*
16. United States v. Robinson, *supra* note 12.
17. United States v. Edwards, 415 U.S. 800 (1974).
18. Schmerber v. California, 384 U.S. 757 (1966).
19. Rochin v. California, 342 U.S. 165 (1952).
20. United States v. Willis, 85 F. Supp. 745 (S. D. Cal. 1949).

86 / SEARCH AND SEIZURE

21. OFFICIAL CODE OF GA. ANN. (O.C.G.A.) §40-6-392.
22. *Id.*
23. O.C.G.A. §40-6-391.
24. Harris v. United States, 390 U.S. 734 (1968); United States v. Lipscomb, 435 F. 2d 780, 795 (5th Cir., 1970); United States v. Gravitt, 484 F. 2d 375, 378 (5th Cir., 1973).
25. United States v. Gravitt, 484 F. 2d 375, 378 (5th Cir., 1973); United States v. Boyd, 436 F. 2d 1203 (1971); United States v. Lipscomb, 435 F. 2d 795 (5th Cir., 1970).
26. Brett v. United States, 412 F. 2d 401 (5th Cir., 1969).
27. Davis v. Mississippi, 394 U.S. 721, 724 (1969).
28. United States v. Jackson, 451 F. 2d 259 (5th Cir., 1971); Redd v. Decker, 447 F. 2d 1346 (5th Cir., 1971).
29. *Id.*
30. Cupp v. Murphy, 412 U.S. 291, 294, 93 S. Ct. 2000, 2003 (1973); Davis v. Mississippi, 394 U.S. 727 (1969).
31. *Id.*
32. Bell v. Wolfish, 441 U.S. 520 (1978).
33. *Id.*
34. *Id.*

13

Searches and Seizures Involving Vehicles

While vehicles and other means of transportation are protected by the Fourth Amendment,[1] their mobility has led to the evolution of several exceptions to the search warrant requirement. Judicial reasoning has been that since a ship, motorboat, airplane, or automobile might quickly be moved out of the jurisdiction of the law enforcement agency, it would be unreasonable to expect officers to use the same constitutional precautions as those required for searching a stationary place such as a home or hotel room.[2]

To give police officers the necessary greater latitude in searching movable vehicles, the courts have termed the mobility factor an exigent circumstance. However, this exigent circumstance alone is not enough to allow a warrantless search of a movable item—there must be probable cause.[3] This exception, which allows the warrantless search of movable vehicles, is commonly known as the **Carroll rule**.[4]

Other exceptions to the search warrant requirement relating to vehicles are mere offshoots of other search and seizure principles covered elsewhere in this book. These include

1. consent searches, (see "Search and Seizure by Consent," p. 71);
2. evidence found within the scope of executing a search warrant (see "What May Be Seized," p. 66);
3. searches incident to an arrest (see "Search Incident to Lawful Arrest," p. 74);
4. inventory or custody searches (see "Searches as a Part of Police Procedure," p. 84); and
5. searching abandoned property (see "Searches of Abandoned Vehicles," p. 93).

STOPPING AND SEARCHING MOVING VEHICLES SUSPECTED OF CARRYING CONTRABAND

A law enforcement officer may stop and search a moving or movable vehicle without a search warrant, provided that prior to the stop there is probable cause to believe that the vehicle contains contraband or other seizable items.[5] This exception, as mentioned earlier, is most often referred to as the Carroll rule. It arose out of a case in which federal agents stopped and searched a vehicle that they had probable cause to believe was carrying "bootleg liquor."[6]

The requirements of a Carroll rule search are

1. that there is probable cause to believe that contraband or other seizable items are in the vehicle and
2. that the vehicle is likely to be moved.[7]

It is unnecessary for the driver or occupants to first be placed under arrest, or for the vehicle to be stopped on the highway.[8] For example, a Carroll rule search was allowed immediately after an automobile was parked in a garage.[9] It is also unnecessary to search the vehicle as soon as it is stopped. The search may be reasonably postponed if at that time it is either impractical to search the vehicle or if the search would endanger the officers.[10]

The key to a Carroll rule search is the existence of probable cause at the time of the search. This qualification makes the warrantless search reasonable. There is probable cause to search a vehicle when existing facts and circumstances are sufficient to lead a reasonably prudent person to believe that the vehicle contains contraband.[11] A mere suspicion is not probable cause,[12] and each case will be decided in light of the particular circumstances.[13] Furthermore, probable cause may not be established from evidence that is found after the search.[14] If incriminating evidence is found in a search that is not supported by probable cause, the search is illegal and the evidence may not be used to obtain a conviction.[15]

Under the Carroll rule, police may search every part of a vehicle being searched, including closed containers that might conceal contraband for which they are looking. However, when probable cause only goes to a particular container within the vehicle, search of the entire vehicle is not justified.[16] Probable cause justifies the search of a lawfully stopped vehicle; it justifies the search of every part of the vehicle and its contents so long as the objects of the search can be concealed therein. A search can be no broader and no narrower than a judge could legitimately authorize by a warrant.[17]

SEARCH OF THE VEHICLE AFTER IT HAS BEEN STOPPED

Assuming that probable cause to justify a Carroll rule search does not exist, other avenues should be considered. If for some reason the vehicle has been stopped,[18] the officer, upon approaching the vehicle, may look for items that are within his or her plain view. (See "Plain View," p. 72, for a detailed discussion of the search aspect.) Since a "police officer is free to seize what he sees in plain sight if he is at a place where he is entitled to be,"[19] the officer may proceed to arrest the occupants upon probable cause derived from the evidence that was in his or her plain view.[20] It should be stressed that an essential element for a "plain view" search and seizure (and any arrest based upon evidence so seized) is that the officer must be within the law when in a position to have a "plain view" of the potential evidence in the first place. (See discussion of plain view on p. 72.) When a highway patrol officer, after requesting to see a tag receipt, shined a flashlight into the glove compartment and saw several plastic bags of a green leafy substance, the officer had probable cause to make an arrest for possession of marijuana.[21]

Another method of searching without a warrant is to obtain consent to search the vehicle. As with any constitutional right, the right to privacy guaranteed by the Fourth Amendment may be knowingly and voluntarily waived.[22] Any incriminating evidence found after valid consent to search has been obtained may be used to gain a conviction.[23]

Since the burden rests upon the state to prove that the evidence was legally seized,[24] either the voluntary relinquishing of keys to the trunk,[25] or the owner's unlocking of the car,[26] makes a stronger case for proving a waiver of the right to privacy. Whether valid consent was obtained is a question ultimately to be decided by the jury who will examine all the circumstances surrounding the consent.[27] Consent should be obtained from the person(s) whose rights against an unreasonable search and seizure are to be protected.[28] Thus, when the owner of the vehicle consents to the search and evidence incriminating someone other than the owner is found, the non-owner cannot contest the search's validity.[29]

SEARCH OF THE VEHICLE FOLLOWING AN ARREST

When an officer has made a valid arrest either under a warrant or upon probable cause that the driver has committed or is committing a crime in his or her presence, the officer may make a complete body search of the driver.[30] (See "Search Incident to a Lawful Arrest," p. 74, and "Search of Person Incident to a Lawful Arrest," p. 82, for further discussion.) The arresting officer may frisk any other occupants of the vehicle not arrested if the nature of the driver's crime makes such a search "reasonable" under the circumstances.[31] To be constitutional, the search of nonarrested occupants must be solely for weapons that might be used to injure the officer or effect an escape. It must not be an exploratory search.[32]

Whenever an arrest is made, the arresting officer has the authority to search the person arrested[33] as well as the immediate vicinity to avoid the possibility of escape, protect the safety of the officer, and prevent the destruction of evidence. The area of search is limited to the vicinity "within the arrestee's immediate control, e.g., that area from within which the arrestee might gain possession of a weapon or destructible evidence."[34] Therefore, a police officer arresting an occupant of an automobile may search the part of the car immediately around and within reach of the arrestee.[35]

The U.S. Supreme Court has recently expanded its interpretation of the area immediately around and within reach of the arrestee to include the entire passenger compartment, including the contents of containers found within, sealed or unsealed. This does **not** include the trunk and, presumably, not the glove compartment.[36] Officers would be well advised to obtain a warrant prior to searching the trunk or glove compartment unless the Carroll rule applies.

A second qualification for constitutionality is that the search must be contemporaneous with the arrest.[37] The search may be started at the scene of the arrest and then continued at some other place as long as "the interval between the beginning and the end of the search was not such as to break the continuity of the search."[38] For example, when a vehicle search was begun at the scene of arrest and police then moved the vehicle one block to headquarters,[39] the search was valid. However, a search that was delayed for two days was held to be unreasonable.[40] When there are no exigent circumstances to justify a delayed search, the officer should take the precaution of obtaining a search warrant for the vehicle.[41]

The last and most elementary requirement of a search incident to an arrest is that the arrest be valid.[42] So any evidence, no matter how incriminating, found in a search pursuant to an illegal arrest (i.e., an arrest without probable cause) may not be used to obtain a conviction.[43]

SEARCHES PURSUANT TO TRAFFIC VIOLATIONS, INVESTIGATORY STOPS, AND ROADBLOCKS

With certain exceptions, there is no right to conduct a search of a vehicle merely because the driver has committed a minor traffic violation.[44] When an officer searched a vehicle, which he had stopped for running a red light, and found untaxed liquor in the trunk, the evidence was held to be inadmissible.[45]

It is often the case, however, that after the initial stop, officers will acquire additional facts that may establish the necessary probable cause for a vehicle search. For example, when officers stopped a vehicle for a traffic violation and saw something thrown under the vehicle just before it stopped, a plain view search was justified. After the officer approached and asked the driver to get out of the car, he smelled the odor of marijuana and saw, in plain view, a rolled cigarette on the floor.[46] In another case, involving a consent search, the driver voluntarily showed his automobile registration documents to a state police officer. The officer noticed that the documents did not correspond to the car's identification number, therefore constituting "improper registration of a motor vehicle."[47]

It is important to remember that if the traffic violation is such that a citation is not issued and the driver is actually placed under custodial arrest, the officer may search the offender[48] as well as the area of the vehicle within the offender's immediate control. (See "Search Incident to a Lawful Arrest," p. 74, "Search of Premises Incident to a Lawful Arrest," p. 78, and "Search of Person Incident to a Lawful Arrest," p. 82.)

The **investigatory stop** also involves the principles of search and seizure. In one case, the Georgia Court of Appeals stated that "policemen have a limited right to momentarily detain citizens for a routine driver's license or identification check which is not an arrest or search and seizure. But this power extends only to that necessary to protect the public."[49]

Officers cannot stop and search just anyone at will. The point at which the routine protection of the public becomes an invasion of the right of privacy of the individual must rest on the particular circumstances involved.[50] Merely being ill-clad and having a "hippie-type" appearance,[51] driving a car not registered on a local college campus,[52] or turning onto a side road after midnight,[53] have been held insufficient to allow for an investigatory stop of the vehicle. On the other hand, instances of driving around in a shopping center long after closing hours,[54] glancing suspiciously back at police through a rear window,[55] traveling at a low speed and weaving across the center line,[56] blinking headlights on and off,[57] or speeding away from police when a preceding vehicle has been stopped[58] have all justified an investigatory stop of the vehicle. From the examples above, it appears that circumstances—time, locality, and behavior of the vehicle's occupants—will be considered by the courts before an investigatory stop of the vehicle is held a valid exercise of police power. Therefore, before making an investigatory stop, the officer should consider whether the facts and circumstances lead to a good faith belief that the activities are sufficiently suspicious to warrant such a stop.[59]

It is important to remember that no one has a right—constitutional or otherwise—to drive a vehicle under any and all circumstances.[60] To ensure that operators are conforming to all driving regulations, the use of roadblocks and test stations have become commonplace.[61] It has been uniformly held that a roadblock to check drivers' licenses, inspection stickers, car registrations, and driver intoxication does not amount to an arrest or search and seizure. Most courts recognize the necessity for roadblocks when not used as a subterfuge for conducting illegal searches and seizures.[62]

While conducting the inspection of the driver and vehicle, the officer may uncover evidence of another crime that will lead to an arrest of the driver or passengers. The leading case in Georgia involved a roadblock of all incoming traffic onto Jekyll Island. The roadblock was manned by a group of city and county law enforcement personnel with a dog trained to sniff marijuana. While checking for expired licenses and inspection stickers, an officer observed marijuana on the floorboard of a vehicle. Believing this to constitute probable cause that contraband was in the vehicle, the officer searched the car—including the glove compartment.[63] (See "Stopping and Searching Moving Vehicles . . . ," p. 88.) The search revealed a quantity of marijuana.

The Supreme Court of Georgia held that while travelers as citizens were entitled to be free from disruption by police officers who were stopping cars in the hopes of uncovering evidence of nontraffic crimes, the momentary stopping for road checks is to be considered reasonable and therefore acceptable.[64] While discovery of the contraband in the glove compartment was not unexpected, the court did not consider the roadblock to be a subterfuge for an illegal search. As long as the roadblock is used to check for expired licenses and inspection stickers and not blatantly as a subterfuge, incriminating evidence uncovered during the momentary detention will be admissible as evidence.

The determination of whether a roadblock is operated as a subterfuge for searching for nontraffic-related offenses is a question of fact to be decided in the trial court. If there is any evidence to support the trial court's opinion that the roadblock is or is not a subterfuge for an illegal search, the decision will not be reversed on appeal.[65]

SEARCHES OF ABANDONED VEHICLES

"It is clear that the personal right to Fourth Amendment protection of property against search and seizure is lost when that property is abandoned."[66]

Whether or not property has been abandoned is largely a question of intent.[67] For purposes of search and seizure of a vehicle, the definition of abandoned property does not require relinquishment of ownership rights.[68] What the officer should consider is whether the owner has abandoned any reasonable expectation of privacy in the vehicle.[69] In determining this, the officer should look at the facts and circumstances behind the owner's abandonment.[70] Courts have held that the owner abandoned a vehicle when

1. owner jumped out of the car, leaving the lights on and the motor running, and attempted to escape from the police.[71]
2. the vehicle was wrecked and left with the door opened.[72]
3. officers searched the trunk of a vehicle found stuck on school premises during the early hours of the morning.[73]
4. a vehicle was illegally parked in a lonely wooded area during the early hours of the morning close to the place where a suspect was being pursued.[74]

A few of the reported cases are so peculiar in nature that their application should be limited to similar factual situations. For example, the courts have held that one abandons the right of privacy in personal property (gambling slips), when one stuffs them behind the rear seat of a police car[75] or when one leaves a "U-Haul" trailer at a service station for three days without first checking with the station owner.[76] The Georgia Court of Appeals held that movable property was abandoned in a case involving a vehicle and trailer that were legally parked on a public street. The vehicle and trailer bore license tags from a county some 70 miles away. Earlier that day, law enforcement officers had arrested an individual who confessed to being from that county, but denied any association with the trailer and vehicle. Officers found a set of keys on the arrested person and, after checking with area residents to determine if any of them owned the vehicles, attempted to open the trailer with the keys. The set of keys fit all the locks and the ensuing search of the vehicles revealed incriminating evidence. The court held that by denying ownership of the vehicles, the owner had abandoned his right of privacy in the property.[77]

A final word of caution should be noted regarding what the courts have termed "forced" or "involuntary" abandonment.[78] If the circumstances are held to be sufficiently compelling to make a person abandon a car involuntarily,[79] then a subsequent search may not be considered a search of an abandoned vehicle. However, the Georgia courts have uniformly held that a suspect's discarding of incriminating evidence[80] or abandoning personal property to make flight easier[81] are not circumstances of involuntary abandonment.

INVENTORY SEARCHES OF VEHICLES TAKEN INTO POLICE CUSTODY

An inventory search of a vehicle includes the searching and listing of all property that belongs to the vehicle's owner. During such a search, any part of the vehicle—the hub caps, glove compartment, and trunk—may be explored for the purpose of finding personal property. The basic reasons for allowing this exception to the search warrant requirement are twofold—(a) to protect the owner's property and (b) to safeguard the police from groundless claims for lost possessions.[82]

Basically there are three situations in which the opportunity for an inventory search may arise:

1. when a vehicle has been impounded and is awaiting forfeiture proceedings. An inventory search in this situation has been held to be valid both in the Georgia and federal courts.[83]

2. when the vehicle has been "taken into custody" for various reasons ranging from obstructing traffic to improper parking. An inventory search in this situation has been held to be valid by the Georgia courts;[84] however, the U.S. Supreme Court has not yet ruled on a case involving an inventory search under these circumstances.[85]
3. when a vehicle has been towed to a private garage at the direction of a police official.

In one case,[86] an off-duty policeman wrecked his vehicle and was later charged with driving while intoxicated. An officer at the scene of the accident directed that the vehicle be towed to a private garage. The following day, a policeman was sent to inventory the vehicle and locate the officer's service revolver. The search of the vehicle revealed evidence that implicated the officer with a recent murder. The evidence was held to be admissible by the U.S. Supreme Court. It should be noted, however, that in reaching its decision, the Court relied more on the principle of plain view than upon the validity of an inventory search.

For the inventory doctrine to be applied, several requirements must be met. First the police must have lawfully obtained custody of the vehicles. This can occur

1. by seizure under a forfeiture statute when a vehicle is found to have been used in conveying contraband.[87]
2. when the vehicle is either the fruit or an instrumentality of a crime,[88] (as when a vehicle was seized and inventoried at the time the defendants were arrested).[89]
3. when the vehicle is impounded for blocking traffic.[90]

Although the courts seem to give a broad interpretation of when a vehicle is blocking traffic, they give no clear guidelines that would be of help to the police.[91]

A second requirement of the valid inventory search is that the inventory be executed under a police regulation,[92] city ordinance, or state statute[93] calling for an inventory to be made of anything taken into police custody. Should a police officer arbitrarily determine which vehicle to inventory, the court may find that the inventory was a mere pretext for a warrantless search.

The third requirement is that police officers may not conduct an inventory search that is obviously an excuse for failing to obtain a search warrant. While the courts have held that the police may harbor an "expectation that contraband might be found in the vehicle,"[94] the same courts have clearly admonished against a pretext search. The courts have recognized the inherent possibility that the police might abuse their inventory power by using it as a pretext to excuse themselves in circumstances where they had unjustifiably failed to secure a search warrant.[95] Should the courts hold that an inventory search was merely a pretext for a warrantless search of the vehicle, any incriminating evidence found during the search would be excluded from the defendant's trial.[96] If it is possible that the court would find an inventory search unjustified, an officer should obtain a warrant before conducting the search.

The fourth and last requirement of an inventory search concerns the scope or areas into which the officer may look while conducting such a search. In considering how far an officer may go in searching a vehicle and still label this activity an inventory search, the officer should recall the reasons for the inventory exception to the search warrant requirement.

Since the inventory is to protect the property of the suspect and to prevent false claims against the police, the areas searched should be limited to carrying out that twofold purpose. While the federal courts have held that a search beneath every seat or in every trunk or glove compartment may not be justified as an inventory,[97] the Georgia courts have been much more liberal in regulating police activity during vehicle inventory searches. The leading Georgia case involved an inventory search of a vehicle impounded for "obstructing a fire lane."[98] During the course of the inventory, an officer opened a letter found inside a folder which was lying on the cutaway of the dashboard. The court held that the several packets of heroin found in the sealed envelope were admissible as evidence under the inventory exception.

SEARCH OF VEHICLES WITH A WARRANT

There are two situations in which an officer may search a vehicle under the authority of a search warrant.

The most common situation is when the vehicle itself is the primary object to be searched. In order to prevent a search warrant from being declared void as a "general search warrant" (e.g., "one which does not sufficiently specify the place. . .to be searched"),[99] the description of the vehicle must be specific enough to permit a prudent officer executing the warrant to be able to locate the vehicle definitely and with reasonable certainty.[100] Thus, when a warrant described the place (vehicle) to be searched as "a 1971 Ford, 4 door sedan, dark green over light green, bearing 1971 Georgia tag, Troup County No. LRK 645 in Houston County, Georgia," the Georgia Court of Appeals held that the description was specific as to the item to be searched and its location—wherever it might be found.[101] The description was not ambiguous merely because it did not recite the vehicle's exact location (i.e., locked up and impounded in a commercial wrecker lot).[102]

The officer must exercise caution in searching the vehicle's occupants at the time the search warrant is executed. If the persons are named or described in the search warrant, clearly they may be searched.[103] Unnamed or undescribed persons do not lose their rights to Fourth Amendment protection by their presence in the named vehicle.[104] However, the officer may search or detain such persons for the limited purpose of self-protection from attack or preventing the concealment or destruction of seizable items.[105]

The second situation arises when a search warrant has been obtained for a particular location (e.g., a home, business, or other building), and upon their arrival to execute the warrant, the officers find a parked vehicle. It has long been the rule in Georgia that a search warrant for a particular location includes the authority to search the curtilage,[106] which is the area often defined as "the enclosed space of ground and buildings immediately surrounding a dwelling house."[107]

In conducting a search of the curtilage, officers may seize items that are not specifically listed in the warrant if "the officers have probable cause to believe the items are tangible evidence of the commission of a crime."[108] When officers, who had a search warrant for stolen liquor believed to be at a specific location, found on the premises a vehicle so loaded that the trunk was only two inches above the ground, the court held that a search of the vehicle was legal. The officers could search the vehicle under the authority of the search warrant for the premises.[109]

In another case where officers had a search warrant for the premises and made a search of a vehicle parked on the curtilage, the court, in holding the search valid, emphasized that the search warrant authorized a search of both the house and lot and that the vehicle was parked very near the house.[110]

However, the officers should not assume that they have blanket authority to search every vehicle which happens to be on the premises. For example, if the officers know that the vehicle will be present on the curtilage and still fail to obtain a search warrant for the vehicle, the courts will be reluctant to permit a search of the vehicle.[111] Officers should exercise caution about searching the vehicles of nonresidents whose presence at the location of the search is merely accidental. In such circumstances, the officers may detain and search the individuals on the premises,[112] but only plain view or consent searches of their vehicles may be conducted.

ENDNOTES

1. Preston v. United States, 376 U.S. 364 (1964).
2. Carroll v. United States, 267 U.S. 132 (1925).
3. Kelley v. State, 129 Ga. App. 131, 198 S.E. 2d 910 (1973); *see* Coolidge v. New Hampshire, 403 U.S. 443, 461-62 (1971), in which the court emphasized that:
   > The word "automobile" is not a talisman in whose presence the Fourth Amendment fades away and disappears. And surely there is nothing in this case to invoke the meaning and purpose of the rule of *Carroll v. United States*—no alerted criminal bent on flight, no fleeing opportunity on an open highway after a hazardous chase, no contraband or stolen goods or weapons, no confederates waiting to move the evidence, not even the inconvenience of a special police detail to guard the immobilized automobile. In short, by no possible stretch of the legal imagination can this be made into a case where "it is not practicable to secure a warrant," and the "automobile exception," despite its label, is simply irrelevant.
4. Carroll v. United States, 267 U.S. 132 (1925).
5. Almeida-Sanchez v. United States, 413 U.S. 266 (1973); Chambers v. Maroney, 399 U.S. 42 (1970); Brinegar v. United States, 338 U.S. 160 (1949); Scher v. United States, 305 U.S. 251 (1938); Husty v. United States, 282 U.S. 694 (1931); Carroll v. United States, 267 U.S. 132 (1925); United States v. Brown, 411 F. 2d 478 (5th Cir. 1969); Williams v. State, 129 Ga. App. 103, 105, 198 S.E. 2d 683 (1973); Johnson v. State, 126 Ga. App. 93, 94, 189 S.E. 2d 900 (1972).
6. Carroll v. United States, 267 U.S. 132 (1925).
7. *Id.*
8. Husty v. United States, 282 U.S. 694 (1931); United States v. Hill, 442 F. 2d 259 (5th Cir. 1971); Anderson v. State, 123 Ga. App. 57, 179 S.E. 286 (1970).
9. Scher v. United States, 305 U.S. 251 (1938). In the Scher case, the officers had probable cause to stop the vehicle on the highway; however, they waited till the car was parked in the owner's opened garage. Upon making a warrantless search of the vehicle, contraband was found and was held to be admissible under the Carroll rule. *See also* Chambers v. Maroney, 399 U.S. 42 (1970).
10. Chambers v. Maroney, 399 U.S. 42 (1970); however, a search eleven months after the seizure of the vehicle is too remote to fall within the Carroll Rule. Coolidge v. New Hampshire, 403 U.S. 443 (1971).
11. United States v. Brown, 411 F. 2d 478 (5th Cir. 1969); Gondor v. State, 129 Ga. App. 665, 200 S.E. 2d 477 (1973); in Carroll v. United States, 267 U.S. 132, 162 (1925), the court explained "probable cause" as:
    > Facts and circumstances within their (the arresting officers') knowl-

edge and of which they had reasonably trustworthy information (which are) sufficient (within) themselves to warrant a man of reasonable caution in the belief that intoxicating liquor (contraband) was being transported in the (vehicle) which they stopped and searched.

12. Gondor v. State, 129 Ga. App. 665, 200 S.E. 2d 477 (1973); Brooks v. State, 129 Ga. App. 109, 198 S.E. 2d 892 (1973).
13. Grimes v. United States, 405 F. 2d 477 (5th Cir. 1968).
14. Henry v. United States, 361 U.S. 98 (1959); Bethea v. State, 127 Ga. App. 97, 192 S.E. 2d 554 (1972); Kelley v. State, 129 Ga. App. 131, 198 S.E. 2d 910 (1973).
15. Garner v. State, 124 Ga. App. 33, 182 S.E. 2d 902 (1971); Kelley v. State, 129 Ga. App. 131, 198 S.E. 2d 910 (1973).
16. U.S. v. Ross, 456 U.S. 798 (1982).
17. *Id.*
18. What authority exists for an officer to make a non-arrest automobile stop? Anderson v. State, 123 Ga. App. 57, 179 S.E. 2d 286 (1970) recognized that:
    In connection with the police power of the state, there is a limited right to speak to and even momentarily detain a citizen for a routine check of driver's license or identification which does not amount to an arrest or a search and seizure, and such right is in itself an invasion of a citizen's right of privacy and is permissible only to the extent that it is necessary to properly safeguard the public welfare.

    However, such "routine investigation" type stops may not be made unless there exists some demonstrable factual reason to lead an officer to have a reasonable suspicion that criminal activity is at hand. L.B.B. v. State, 129 Ga. App. 163, 198 S.E. 2d 895 (1973). *See,* "Non-Arrest Automobile Stops: Unconstitutional Seizures of the Person," 25 *Stan. L. Rev.* 865 (1973).
19. Brewer v. State, 129 Ga. App. 118, 199 S.E. 2d 109 (1973).
20. Bass v. State, 123 Ga. App. 705, 182 S.E. 2d 322 (1971).
21. Caito v. State, 130 Ga. App. 831, 204 S.E. 2d 765 (1974).
22. Zap v. United States, 328 U.S. 624 (1946); United States v. Fike, 449 F. 2d 191 (5th Cir. 1971); Guest v. State, 230 Ga. 569, 198 S.E. 2d 158 (1973); Morrison v. State, 129 Ga. App. 558, 200 S.E. 2d 286 (1973); Tanner v. State, 114 Ga. App. 35, 150 S.E. 2d 189 (1966).
23. Young v. State, 113 Ga. App. 497, 148 S.E. 2d 461 (1966); Barron v. State, 109 Ga. App. 786, 137 S.E. 2d 690 (1964).
24. Traylor v. State, 127 Ga. App. 409, 193 S.E. 2d 876 (1972).
25. Strickland v. State, 226 Ga. 750, 177 S.E. 2d 238 (1970).
26. Young v. State, 113 Ga. App. 497, 148 S.E. 2d 461 (1966).
27. This is a "totality of the circumstances test where the court looks at such factors as the age of the suspect, level of education, length of detention, and whether coercion—expressed or implied—was used on the suspect." Merrill v. State, 130 Ga. App. 745, 204 S.E. 2d 632 (1974). Threatening to obtain a search warrant when a suspect is alone, frightened, and upset has been held to be coercive. Flournoy v. State, 205 S.E. 2d 473 (1974).
28. Goldstein v. United States, 316 U.S. 114 (1941).
29. Alderman v. United States, 394 U.S. 165 (1969); Grantling v. State, 229 Ga. 746, 194 S.E. 2d 405 (1972); Strickland v. State, 226 Ga. 750, 177 S.E. 2d 238 (1970); Marsh v. State, 223 Ga. 590, 157 S.E. 2d 273 (1967).

100 / SEARCH AND SEIZURE

30. United States v. Robinson, 414 U.S. 218, (1973); Gustafson v. Florida, 414 U.S. 260 (1973); OFFICIAL CODE OF GA. ANN. (O.C.G.A.) §17-5-1.
31. Terry v. Ohio, 392 U.S. 1 (1968); L.B.B. v. State, 129 Ga. App. 163, 198 S.E. 2d 895 (1973).
32. Whether a search of a nonoccupant is reasonable will be decided by the court after looking at all the factual circumstances surrounding the case. Roach v. State, 221 Ga. 783, 147 S.E. 2d 299 (1966). Certainly a key factor that the court will look for is information or facts that would reasonably lead the officer to believe that the occupant might be armed and dangerous. Bethea v. State, 127 Ga. App. 97, 192 S.E. 2d 554 (1972). If the arrest was made with a warrant or the officer had a search warrant for the vehicle, the officer could detain and search any occupant in the vehicle. O.C.G.A. §17-5-28.
33. United States v. Robinson, 414 U.S. 218 (1973); Gustafson v. Florida, 414 U.S. 260 (1973).
34. Chimel v. California, 395 U.S. 752, 762-63 (1969).
35. Such areas as the trunk or the motor compartment may not be searched under the principle of "search incident to an arrest." Rowland v. State, 117 Ga. App. 577, 161 S.E. 2d 422 (1968); *Annon.,* 10 A.L.R. 3d 314; 19 A.L.R. 3d 727; 68 Am. Jur. 2d. *Search and Seizures* §96 (1973). However, if the arrest is of such a nature as to allow for a Carroll rule search (see p. 87), then the arresting officer may search all areas of the vehicle where hidden contraband might be found. United States v. Newsome, 432 F. 2d 51 (5th Cir. 1970).
36. New York v. Belton, 453 U.S. 454 (1980).
37. Preston v. United States, 376 U.S. 364 (1964); Coolidge v. New Hampshire, 403 U.S. 443 (1971); Hunter v. State, 127 Ga. App. 664, 194 S.E. 2d 680 (1972).
38. Crone v. United States, 411 F. 2d 251 (5th Cir. 1969); *cert. denied,* Chontos v. United States, 396 U.S. 896 (1969).
39. *Id.*
40. Coolidge v. New Hampshire, 403 U.S. 443 (1971).
41. United States v. Altizer, 477 F. 2d 846 (5th Cir. 1973).
42. Traylor v. State, 127 Ga. App. 409, 193 S.E. 2d 876 (1972).
43. Kelley v. State, 129 Ga. App. 131, 198 S.E. 2d 910 (1973).
44. Rowland v. State, 117 Ga. App. 577, 161 S.E. 2d 422 (1968); Annon., 10 A.L.R. 3d 314 (1966).
45. *Id.*
46. United States v. Baty, 486 F. 2d 240 (5th Cir. 1973); Hood v. State, 229 Ga. 435, 192 S.E. 2d 154 (1972); Shearer v. State, 128 Ga. App. 809, 198 S.E. 2d 369 (1973); Dickson v. State, 124 Ga. App. 406, 184 S.E. 2d 37 (1971).
47. Hart v. United States, 316 F. 2d 916 (5th Cir. 1963).
48. United States v. Robinson, 414 U.S. 218 (1973); Gustafson v. Florida, 414 U.S. 260 (1973).
49. Anderson v. State, 123 Ga. App. 57, 179 S.E. 2d 286 (1970).
50. Anderson v. State, 123 Ga. App. 57, 61, 179 S.E. 2d 286, 289 (1970). This is not a novel principle of law laid down by the courts. The case of Terry v. Ohio, 392 U.S. 1 (1968), was instrumental in granting the police a right to investigate where there were suspicious circumstances. The application of Terry to individuals sitting in a parked car was made in Adams v. Williams, 407 U.S. 143 (1972). However, the viewpoint of the individual citizen who may be offended by such accosting can be found in Reich, "Police Questioning of Law Abiding Citizens," 75 *Yale L. J.* 1161 (1966), which has been cited and referred to in Anderson v. State, 123 Ga. App. 57, 61, 179 S.E. 2d 286, 289

(1970); Davidson v. State, 125 Ga. App. 502, 505, 188 S.E. 2d 124 (1972); and Papachristou v. City of Jacksonville, 405 U.S. 156 (1972).
51. Bethea v. State, 127 Ga. App. 97, 192 S.E. 2d 554 (1972).
52. Davidson v. State, 125 Ga. App. 502, 188 S.E. 2d 124 (1972).
53. Brooks v. State, 129 Ga. App. 109, 198 S.E. 2d 892 (1973).
54. Anderson v. State, 123 Ga. App. 57, 179 S.E. 2d 286 (1970).
55. Lofton v. State, 122 Ga. App. 727, 178 S.E. 2d 693 (1970).
56. Nicholson v. United States, 355 F. 2d 80 (5th Cir. 1966); *cert. denied,* 384 U.S. 974 (1966).
57. Hogan v. Atkins, 411 F. 2d 576 (5th Cir. 1969).
58. Williams v. State, 129 Ga. App. 103, 198 S.E. 2d 683 (1973).
59. L.B.B. v. State, 129 Ga. App. 163, 198 S.E. 2d 895 (1973).
60. Swift v. State, 131 Ga. App. 231, 206 S.E. 2d 51 (1974), dissenting opinion, J. Hall.
61. 7 Am. Jur. 2d *Automobiles* §98 (1963); O.C.G.A. §17-4-23 provides that any law enforcement officer may arrest persons for violating any law, regulation, or ordinance respecting vehicles when the offense occurs in his presence.
62. 7 Am. Jur. 2d *Automobiles* §98 (1963); Swift v. State, 131 Ga. App. 231, 206 S.E. 2d 51 (1974); rev'd State v. Swift, 232 Ga. 535, 207 S.E. 2d 459 (1974); Anderson v. State, 123 Ga. App. 57, 179 S.E. 2d 286 (1970); *see* Reich, "Police Questioning of Law Abiding Citizens," 75 Yale L. J. 1161 (1966).
63. Chambers v. Maroney, 399 U.S. 42 (1970).
64. State v. Swift, 232 Ga. 535, 207 S.E. 2d 459 (1974).
65. *Id.*
66. United States v. Edwards, 441 F. 2d 749, 752 (5th Cir. 1971).
67. Croker v. State, 114 Ga.App. 43, 150 S.E. 2d 294 (1966).
68. Jones v. United States, 362 U.S. 257 (1960).
69. Jones v. United States, 362 U.S. 257 (1960); United States v. Edwards, 441 F. 2d 745 (5th Cir. 1971); United States v. Ventresca, 380 U.S. 102 (1965).
70. Croker v. State, 114 Ga. App. 43, 150 S.E. 2d 294 (1966).
71. United States v. Edwards, 441 F. 2d 749 (5th Cir. 1971); Whitlock v. State, 124 Ga. App. 599, 185 S.E. 2d 90 (1971).
72. Grimes v. United States, 405 F. 2d 477 (5th Cir. 1968).
73. Craft v. State, 124 Ga. App. 57, 183 S.E. 2d 37 (1971).
74. Hunter v. State, 127 Ga. App. 664, 194 S.E. 2d 680 (1972).
75. United States v. Maryland, 479 F. 2d 566 (5th Cir. 1973).
76. United States v. Gulledge, 469 F. 2d 713 (5th Cir. 1972).
77. Croker v. State, 114 Ga. App. 43, 150 S.E. 2d 294 (1966).
78. *See* United States v. Colbert, 474 F. 2d 174, 186 (5th Cir. 1973).
79. United States v. Edwards, 441 F. 2d 749, 753 (5th Cir. 1971).
80. Green v. State, 127 Ga. App. 713, 194 S.E. 2d 678 (1972).
81. Whitlock v. State, 124 Ga. App. 599, 185 S.E. 2d 90 (1971).
82. Harris v. United States, 390, U.S. 234, 236 (1968); United States v. Edwards, 441 F. 2d 749 (5th Cir. 1971); United States v. Kelehar, 470 F. 2d 176 (5th Cir. 1972).

83. Cooper v. California, 386 U.S. 58 (1967); Morrison v. State, 129 Ga. App. 558, 200 S.E. 2d 286 (1973).
84. Denson v. State, 128 Ga. App. 456, 197 S.E. 2d 156 (1973).
85. *See* "Comment, Police Inventories of the Contents of Vehicles and the Exclusionary Rule," 29 *Wash. and Lee L. Rev.* 197 (1972). Should the high court hold inventory searches of vehicles impounded merely for minor traffic offenses unconstitutional, the effect of such a decision would be to reverse Denson v. State, *supra,* note 84, which is the Georgia decision validating the inventory search in the "traffic offense" situation.
86. Cady v. Dombrowski, 413 U.S. 433 (1973).
87. For example, the condemnation of a vehicle used to transport a prohibited drug, O.C.G.A. §§16-14-49, 27-3-2,3, or a vehicle used to shoot deer at night, O.C.G.A. §27-3-45.
88. O.C.G.A. §17-5-1.
89. United States v. Gravitt, 484 F. 2d 375 (5th Cir. 1973).
90. Denson v. State, 128 Ga. App. 456, 197 S.E. 2d 156 (1973).
91. Hansen v. State, 168 Ga. App. 304, 308 S.E. 2d 236 (1983).
92. Many of the cases, while not citing a specific police regulation, have made reference in the facts that the police were merely conforming to their regulations by conducting an inventory search of the vehicle. *See* United States v. Gravitt, 484 F. 2d 375, 380 (5th Cir. 1973) (standard operating procedure); United States v. Kelehar, 470 F. 2d 176, 178 (5th Cir. 1972) (within the bounds of standard inventory procedure); Denson v. State, 128 Ga. App. 456, 197 S.E. 2d 156 (1973) (in compliance with standard inventory procedure).
93. O.C.G.A. §17-5-2 reads:
    An inventory of all instruments, articles or things seized on a search without a warrant shall be given to the person arrested and a copy thereof delivered to the judicial officer before whom the person arrested is taken. If the person arrested is released without a charge being preferred against him all instruments, articles or things seized, other than contraband or stolen property, shall be returned to him upon release.
94. United States v. Kelehar, 470 F. 2d 176 (5th Cir. 1972).
95. United States v. Gravitt, 484 F. 2d 375, 380 (5th Cir. 1973).
96. Mapp v. Ohio, 367 U.S. 643 (1961).
97. United States v. Gravitt, 484 F. 2d 375, 381 (5th Cir. 1973).
98. Denson v. State, 128 Ga. App. 456, 197 S.E. 2d 158 (1973).
99. Willis v. State, 122 Ga. App. 455, 177 S.E. 2d 487 (1970).
100. Steele v. United States, 267 U.S. 498 (1925); Reed v. State, 126 Ga. App. 323, 190 S.E. 2d 587 (1972); Fomby v. State, 120 Ga. App. 387, 170 S.E. 2d 585, 587 (1969); Steele v. State, 118 Ga. App. 433, 434, 164 S.E. 2d 255, 256 (1968).
101. Reed v. State, 126 Ga. App. 323, 190 S.E. 2d 587 (1972).
102. *Id.*
103. Wood v. State, 224 Ga. 121, 160 S.E. 2d 368 (1968).
104. United States v. Di Re, 332 U.S. 581 (1948).
105. O.C.G.A. §17-5-28, Wood v. State, 224 Ga. 121, 160 S.E. 2d 368 (1968).
106. Daniels v. State, 78 Ga. 98 (1866); Moon v. State, 120 Ga. App. 141, 169 S.E. 2d 632 (1969); Hutchins v. State, 3 Ga. App. 300, 59 S.E. 848 (1907).

107. *Black's Law Dictionary*, 460 (4th ed. 1951); Wright v. State, 12 Ga. App. 514, 77 S.E. 657 (1913).
108. Campbell v. State, 226 Ga. 883, 178 S.E. 2d 257 (1970).
109. Thompson v. State, 230 Ga. 610, 198 S.E. 2d 288 (1973).
110. Brooks v. United States, 416 F. 2d 1044 (5th Cir. 1969).
111. Coolidge v. New Hampshire, 403 U.S. 443 (1971).
112. O.C.G.A. §17-5-28.

14

Electronic Surveillance as Search and Seizure

Invasions of privacy by electronic surveillance involve a third party's secret interception of an otherwise private conversation without the consent of a party to the conversation. Electronic surveillance may take the form of wiretapping, interception of conversations by concealed transmission devices (bugs), or other forms of surveillance.

In this discussion, the term **eavesdropping** will be used to include all types of electronic surveillance. This chapter will clarify what conversations are protected against eavesdropping, explain the procedure for obtaining and executing an investigative warrant, and point out the limitations on a warrant and the exceptions to the warrant requirement.

CONVERSATIONS ARE PROTECTED

The Fourth Amendment requirement that searches and seizures by police officials be reasonable applies not only to the seizure of tangible items, but to the recording or interception of oral statements as well.[1] Until recently, however, this has not been the rule. In earlier decisions, the U.S. Supreme Court held that the interception of conversations was not an unreasonable search and seizure.[2] The Fourth Amendment did not protect conversations alone. Police officials would have to seize papers or other tangible items or make an actual physical invasion of the building or curtilage for individuals to gain Fourth Amendment protection.[3]

For example, when police officials tapped a phone in the basement of an office building, the Court held that there was no search and seizure.[4] The Court emphasized that without an actual physical intrusion into the premises where the conversations were taking place, there could be no search within Fourth Amendment protection. Likewise, there was found to be no search when policemen placed a listening device against a wall for the purpose of overhearing a conversation in the adjoining room.[5] However, when a "spike mike" was driven through a common wall until it hit a heating duct in the house used by the suspects, the Court found that there had been sufficient physical intrusion into the premises to constitute a trespass.[6] In this case, the interception of the conversations was found to be unreasonable search, and thus illegal.

In more recent cases, the requirement that there be an actual physical invasion of the premises in order to constitute a search has been abandoned. *The Supreme Court has now held that every electronic eavesdropping upon a private conversation is a search and seizure.*[7] The practical effect of this rule is that in all cases where the police use any form of electronic eavesdropping to intercept conversations, they must first obtain an investigative warrant. Except in a limited number of circumstances, any eavesdropping done without a warrant is illegal.

INVESTIGATIVE WARRANT REQUIREMENT

While both Georgia[8] and the federal government[9] have laws that regulate electronic eavesdropping, this discussion will be limited to the Georgia provisions. The Georgia statute makes it unlawful for any person to invade another's privacy by secretly intercepting a private conversation or observing another's activities.[10] The statute provides an exception for law enforcement officers enabling them to engage in electronic eavesdropping under the authority of an investigative warrant.

An investigative warrant may be issued by any judge of the superior court of the circuit where the warrant is to be executed. Upon a written application to the judge by the attorney general or by the district attorney of the place where the surveillance is to take place, the judge determines whether there is probable cause to believe that

1. a crime is being or has been committed, or
2. a private place is being used for the commission of that crime.[11]

The judge bases the determination of probable cause on factors similar to those discussed in the section on search warrants. (See

Chapter 9.) The application must contain enough facts to enable the judge to determine that there is probable cause for a warrant. The application must also cite the eavesdropping devices to be used and the specific conversations and activities to be overheard or observed.[12]

Execution of the Warrant

The Georgia legislature has shown its concern for protecting the individual's right of privacy by placing strict controls on the execution of an investigative warrant so that it is even more closely regulated than that of an ordinary search warrant. An investigative warrant may be issued for no more than 20 days. However, unlike an ordinary search warrant, the investigative warrant may be renewed for good cause.[13] If the warrant is not renewed, it may not be used to justify any eavesdropping activities which took place after the expiration of the 20-day period.

After executing it, the officer must write on the warrant how it was used and what information was obtained as a result of the surveillance. Upon returning the warrant to the judge who issued it, the officer must state that the investigation was performed in accordance with the terms of the warrant and that the surveillance was terminated immediately after the information authorized by the warrant was obtained.[14]

Exceptions to the Warrant Requirement

Under Georgia law a party may consent to having his or her conversations intercepted. If police officials have the consent of one party, they may intercept the conversation without obtaining an investigative warrant.[15] The consent exception is frequently used when an informant or undercover agent engages a suspect in conversation and either records or transmits their conversation through a concealed electronic device.

It has been held that when an informant transmits a conversation with a police suspect by use of a concealed electronic device, the Fourth Amendment is not violated.[16] The reasoning behind this decision was that those who engage in crime are not protected from the risk that their associates will cooperate with the police.[17] This same rationale can be used to permit an informant to record a conversation with a suspect.[18] Police officials may also "bug" a person's office, or other private place, when they have the person's consent, and they may intercept messages although they have not obtained an investigative warrant.[19]

Without obtaining an investigative warrant, police officials may use flashlights, searchlights, binoculars, or similar devices to observe the activities of others.[20] These devices are not used to eavesdrop in the usual manner, but rather to secretly watch the activities of criminal suspects. As long as the observing officers are in a place where they are entitled to be, they may watch any activities which are in plain view. This plain view exception is not destroyed by the fact that such equipment is used to aid the officers' sight.

ENDNOTES

1. Katz v. United States, 389 U.S. 347, 353 (1967).
2. Goldman v. United States, 316 U.S. 129 (1942); Olmstead v. United States, 277 U.S. 438 (1928).
3. *Id.*
4. Olmstead v. United States, 277 U.S. 438 (1928).
5. Goldman v. United States, 316 U.S. 129 (1942).
6. Silverman v. United States, 365 U.S. 505 (1961).
7. Desist v. United States, 394 U.S. 244 (1969).
8. OFFICIAL CODE OF GA. ANN. (O.C.G.A.) §§16-11-60 through 69.
9. 18 U.S.C.A. §2510-20 (1970).
10. O.C.G.A. §16-11-62.
11. O.C.G.A. §16-11-64(b)(1).
12. O.C.G.A. §16-11-64.
13. O.C.G.A. §16-11-64(b)(3).
14. O.C.G.A. §16-11-64(b)(4).
15. O.C.G.A. §16-11-66.
16. On Lee v. United States, 343 U.S. 747 (1952), *rev'd on other grounds;* White v. United States, 401 U.S. 745 (1971).
17. Hoffa v. United States, 385 U.S. 293, 302 (1966); White v. United States, 401 U.S. 745, 749 (1971).
18. Lopez v. United States, 373 U.S. 427 (1963).
19. Ansley v. State, 124 Ga. App. 670, 185 S.E. 2d 562 (1971).
20. O.C.G.A. §16-11-60. *See also* Green v. State, 250 Ga. 610, 299 S.E. 2d 544 (1983).

15

Effects of an Illegal Search and Seizure

Chapters 9 and 10 discussed the requirements for a reasonable search and seizure and the exceptions to the search warrant requirement. To give full effect to the Fourth Amendment requirement that searches and seizures be reasonable, both state and federal governments[1] have created rules that allow illegally seized evidence to be suppressed. Thus, the first result of an illegal search and seizure is that the evidence seized during an illegal search may be excluded from the defendant's trial. However, the **exclusionary rule** does not immunize a defendant from criminal prosecution; it simply prohibits the prosecution from introducing the illegally seized evidence in the defendant's trial.

Georgia law[2] allows the defendant whose property has been illegally seized to request that the evidence be suppressed on the following grounds:

1. The search and seizure with a warrant was illegal because (a) the warrant was insufficient on its face, (b) there was not probable cause for issuance of the warrant, or (c) the warrant was illegally executed.
2. The search and seizure without a warrant was illegal.

ILLEGAL SEARCHES WITH A WARRANT

When a warrant is required to conduct a search, it must be legally issued, and it must be executed according to its terms. Evidence seized under the authority of an illegally issued or executed search warrant can be suppressed at the trial.[3] Trial judges have specific guidelines to follow in determining whether a search warrant was legally issued. These guidelines are described in Chapter 9 and include such things as whether an affidavit was properly filed, whether an authorized judicial officer issued the warrant, and whether the warrant contained precise descriptions of the places or persons to be searched and the things to be seized.

However, mere technical irregularities will not invalidate the warrant.[4] Although the Georgia courts have not considered the requirement that the affidavit contain a statement concerning the time of occurrence of the facts to be merely technical, it was held that a warrant was valid when it contained only the date of issuance and not the hour.[5] But if the warrant does not include the time element, the evidence seized will be suppressed.[6]

If the warrant is illegally executed, the evidence seized as a result of the illegal search can be excluded. For example, evidence seized at a residence not described in the warrant was inadmissible, even though officers knew that the description was in error. In fact, they searched the premises that should have been described in the warrant.[7] Likewise, if a search warrant is not executed at a reasonable time or at the time specified in the warrant, the evidence seized during the search can be suppressed.[8]

ILLEGAL SEARCHES WITHOUT A WARRANT

There are limited situations in which a police officer may conduct a warrantless search and seizure. Even though a warrant is not required, the search and seizure must strictly conform to the requirements set out in Chapter 10. Strict compliance with these rules is not excused simply because a warrant is not required. If an officer exceeds the bounds of a warrantless search, any evidence seized may be suppressed. Evidence seized pursuant to a warrantless search was suppressed when the officer's search for the evidence preceded the arrest and served as its justification.[9]

The court also showed concern for strict compliance with the requirements of a warrantless search when it suppressed evidence seized under an illegal plain view search. In this case police officials conducted a general exploratory search of the defendant's car until they found the incriminating evidence.[10]

PERSONAL LIABILITY FOR ILLEGAL SEARCH AND SEIZURE

The Fourth Amendment and federal statutes[11] guarantee

the right of every individual to be free from illegal searches and seizures. To protect these guarantees, the courts allow a private citizen to sue for damages when that citizen or citizen's property has been subject to an illegal search or seizure. The injured person may bring a civil suit against the police official who has engaged in this unlawful activity.

The U.S. Supreme Court has held that the Fourth Amendment allows a private citizen to bring a suit for deprivation of his or her constitutional rights against a federal law enforcement officer. Thus, the Court allowed a citizen's damage suit for injuries sustained as a result of an illegal search and seizure by federal narcotics agents.[12] Under the federal statute[13] the Court permitted a damage suit against state officers when they did not act in good faith in going to the suspect's home and conducting a search without a warrant.[14] Another federal statute[15] allows any person whose wire or oral communications are unlawfully intercepted to sue for damages.

Georgia law provides that municipal officers shall be personally liable to persons who sustain damages as a result of their official acts.[16] Thus, a police officer may be sued for money damages on the grounds that the officer conducted an illegal search and seizure.

While the individual officer may be sued for injuries caused by an illegal search and seizure, this liability does not extend to the municipality. Georgia law provides specifically that municipalities shall not be liable for the illegal acts of police officers engaged in the discharge of their duties.[17]

Consent — A Defense to Personal Liability

If an individual voluntarily consents to a search of his or her property, then the police official who conducted the search may raise the suspect's consent as a defense to any suit for damages against that official. As a general rule, a search without a warrant is unreasonable, but a consent search is a recognized exception to the warrant requirement. A suspect who consents to a warrantless search is said to have waived the right to have a search of his or her property conducted pursuant to a warrant.[18] However, it must be clear from all the circumstances of the case that the suspect consented freely without coercion by the police officers. (See "Search and Seizure by Consent" p. 71.)

ENDNOTES

1. Mapp v. Ohio, 367 U.S. 643 (1961); Paige v. State, 219 Ga. 569, 572, 134 S.E. 2d 793, 796 (1964).
2. OFFICIAL CODE OF GA. ANN. (O.C.G.A.) §17-5-30.
3. O.C.G.A. §17-5-30(a)(2).
4. O.C.G.A. §17-5-31.
5. Merritt v. State, 121 Ga. App. 832, 833, 175 S.E. 2d 890, 892 (1970).
6. Fowler v. State, 121 Ga. App. 22, 172 S.E. 2d 449 (1970).
7. Bell v. State, 124 Ga. App. 139, 182 S.E. 2d 901 (1971).
8. O.C.G.A. §17-5-26.
9. Kelley v. State, 129 Ga. App. 131, 198 S.E. 2d 910 (1973).
10. Mobley v. State, 130 Ga. App. 80, 202 S.E. 2d 465 (1973).
11. 42 U.S.C.A. §1983 (1970).
12. Bivens v. Six Unknown Named Agents of Federal Bureau of Narcotics, 403 U.S. 388 (1971).
13. 42 U.S.C.A. §1983 (1970).
14. Caperci v. Huntoon, 397 F. 2d 799 (1st Cir. 1968); *cert. denied,* 393 U.S. 940 (1968).
15. 18 U.S.C.A. §2520 (1970).
16. O.C.G.A. §36-33-4.
17. O.C.G.A. §36-33-3.
18. United States v. Five Gambling Devices, 119 F. Supp. 641 (D.C. Ga. 1952).

Table of Cases

Note: The numbers following each case refer to the footnote and page numbers. The first number(s) indicates the footnote number of the specific case. The number enclosed in parentheses is the page number of text on which the case is discussed.

—A—

Adams v. State, 121 Ga. 163, 165, 48 S.E. 910, 911 (1904) . . . 1, 3, 7 (35)
Adams v. Williams, 407 U.S. 143 (1972) . . . 4 (82), 50 (92)
Aguilar v. Texas, 378 U.S. 108 (1964) . . . 43, 44, 45 (12), 40 (63)
Alderman v. United States, 394 U.S. 165 (1969) . . . 29 (89)
Alexander v. State, 225 Ga. 358, 360, 168 S.E. 2d 315, 317 (1969) . . . 13 (4), 10 (82)
Almeida-Sanchez v. United States, 413 U.S. 266 (1973) . . . 5 (88)
Anderson v. State, 123 Ga. App. 57, 61, 179 S.E. 2d 286, 289 (1970) . . . 19 (72), 8 (88), 18 (89), 49 (91), 50, 54, 62 (92)
Ansley v. State, 124 Ga. App. 670, 185 S.E. 2d 562 (1971) . . . 19 (106)

—B—

Barnwell v. State, 127 Ga. App. 335, 193 S.E. 2d 203 (1972) . . . 7 (3), 8 (4)
Barron v. State, 109 Ga. App. 786, 787-88, 137 S.E. 2d 690, 693 (1964) . . . 3 (3), 23 (89)
Bass v. State, 123 Ga. App. 705, 182 S.E. 2d 322 (1971) . . . 20 (89)
Bell v. State, 124 Ga. App. 139, 140, 182 S.E. 2d 901 (1971) . . . 15 (60), 16 (61), 7 (109)
Bell v. State, 128 Ga. App. 426, 427, 196 S.E. 2d 894, 895 (1973) . . . 48 (13)
Bell v. Wolfish, 441 U.S. 520 (1978) . . . 32, 33, 34 (85)
Berger v. New York, 388 U.S. 41, 53, 55 (1967) . . . 1 (57), 29 (74)
Bethea v. State, 127 Ga. App. 97, 192 S.E. 2d 554 (1972) . . . 12 (4), 39, 44 (75), 13 (83), 14 (88), 32 (90), 51 (92)
Bivens v. Six Unknown Named Agents of Federal Bureau of Narcotics, 403 U.S. 388 (1971) . . . 12 (110)
Blair v. State, 90 Ga. 326, 330, 17 S.E. 96, 97 (1892) . . . 80 (16), 52, 53 (25), 9 (51)
Blake v. State, 109 Ga. App. 636, 641, 642, 137 S.E. 2d 49, 53 (1964) . . . 26, 27 (45)
Blocker v. Clark, 126 Ga. 484, 486-87, 488-89, 490, 54 S.E. 1022, 1023-24 (1906) . . . 12 (8), 13 (9), 69, 70, 71 (15), 23 (45)
Bostwick v. State, 124 Ga. App. 113, 182 S.E. 2d 925 (1971) . . . 77 (67)
Brady v. Davis, 9 Ga. 73, 75 (1850) . . . 6 (7)

114 / ARREST/SEARCH AND SEIZURE

Braddock v. State, 127 Ga. App. 513, 517-18, 194 S.E. 2d 317, 320 (1972) ... 15 (72)
Brett v. United States, 412 F. 2d 401 (5th Cir. 1969) ... 26 (84)
Brewer v. State, 129 Ga. App. 118, 199 S.E. 2d 109 (1973) ... 17, 18 (72), 19 (89)
Brinegar v. United States, 338 U.S. 160, 175-76 (1949) ... 29 (74), 5 (88)
Britt v. Davis, 130 Ga. 74, 77, 60 S.E. 180, 181 (1908) ... 58 (14)
Brooks v. State, 114 Ga. 6, 7, 8, 39 S.E. 877, 878 (1901) ... 9, 19 (21)
Brooks v. State, 129 Ga. App. 109, 111, 198 S.E. 2d 892, 894 (1973) ... 3 (81), 12 (88), 53 (92)
Brooks v. State, 129 Ga. App. 393, 199 S.E. 2d 578 (1973) ... 9 (80)
Brooks v. United States, 416 F. 2d 1044 (5th Cir. 1969) ... 110 (97)
Brunswick & Western R.R. v. Ponder, 117 Ga. 63, 66, 43 S.E. 430, 431 (1903) ... 39 (38)
Buck v. State, 127 Ga. App. 72, 73, 74, 192 S.E. 2d 432, 434 (1972) ... 43, 44, 45 (12), 10 (60), 40, 42, 44 (63)
Bumper v. North Carolina, 391 U.S. 543 (1968) ... 9 (72)
Bundy v. State, 168 Ga. App. 90, 91, 308 S.E. 2d 213, 215 (1983) ... 66 (66)
Burns v. State, 119 Ga. App. 678, 168 S.E. 2d 786 (1969) ... 45 (12)

—C—

Cady v. Dombrowski, 413 U.S. 433 (1973) ... 32 (74), 86 (95)
Caito v. State, 130 Ga. App. 831, 204 S.E. 2d 765 (1974) ... 20 (73), 21 (89)
Campbell v. State, 226 Ga. 883, 178 S.E. 2d 257 (1970) ... 46 (12), 34 (62), 108 (97)
Cannon v. Grimes, 223 Ga. 35, 36, 153 S.E. 2d 445, 446 (1967) ... 5 (43)
Cantrell v. Mayor & Council of Mt. Airy, 218 Ga. 646, 129 S.E. 2d 910 (1963) ... 54 (25), 10 (51)
Caperci v. Huntoon, 397 F. 2d 799 (1st Cir. 1968), *cert. denied* 393 U.S. 940 (1968) ... 14 (110)
Carroll v. United States, 267 U.S. 132, 149, 162 (1925) ... 29, 36 (74), 2, 3, 4 (87), 5, 6, 7, 11 (88)
Carson v. State, 221 Ga. 299, 144 S.E. 2d 384 (1965) ... 39, 40 (63)
Chambers v. Maroney, 399 U.S. 42 (1970) ... 26 (73), 5, 9, 10 (88), 63 (92)
Chapman v. United States, 365 U.S. 610 (1961) ... 11 (72), 35 (74)
Chimel v. California, 395 U.S. 752, 762-63 (1969) ... 2 (57), 2, 3 (71), 5 (79), 34 (90)
Chontos v. United States, 396 U.S. 896 (1969) ... 38, 39 (90)
Cleland v. United States Fidelity and Guar. Ins. Co., 99 Ga. App. 130, 107 S.E. 2d 904 (1959) ... 22 (9), 76 (16)
Clement v. State, 226 Ga. 66, 172 S.E. 2d 600 (1970) ... 16 (4)

Cobb v. Bailey, 35 Ga. App. 302, 133 S.E. 42 (1926) . . . 31, 32 (23), 11 (31)
Coker v. State, 14 Ga. App. 606, 81 S.E. 818 (1914) . . . 80 (16), 52 (25), 9 (51)
Coleman v. State, 121 Ga. 594, 597, 49 S.E. 716, 717 (1905) . . . 1 (30), 20 (32)
Connolly v. Thurber Whyland Co., 92 Ga. 651, 654, 18 S.E. 1004, 1005 (1983) . . . 2 (43)
Conoly v. Imperial Tobacco Co., 63 Ga. App. 880, 885, 12 S.E. 2d 398, 403 (1940) . . . 1 (3), 5 (3)
Coolidge v. New Hampshire, 403 U.S. 443 (1971) . . . 2, 3 (57), 24 (61), 13 (72), 23, 26 (73), 30 (74), 3 (87), 10 (88), 37, 40 (90), 111 (98)
Cooper v. California, 386 U.S. 58 (1967) . . . 83 (94)
Cooper v. Lunsford, 203 Ga. 166, 174, 45 S.E. 2d 395, 400 (1947) . . . 72, 75 (16)
Courtoy v. Dozier, 20 Ga. 369 (1856) . . . 6 (3)
Cox v. Perkins, 151 Ga. 632, 107 S.E. 863 (1921) . . . 26 (10), 63 (15), 30 (62)
Craft v. State, 124 Ga. App. 57, 183 S.E. 2d 37 (1971) . . . 73 (93)
Creamer v. State, 150 Ga. App. 458, 258 S.E. 2d 212 (1979) . . . 35 (23)
Croker v. State, 114 Ga. App. 43, 150 S.E. 2d 294 (1966) . . . 67, 70, 77 (93)
Croker v. State, 114 Ga. App. 492, 494, 151 S.E. 2d 846, 848 (1966) . . . 25 (22), 24 (32), 1, 6 (35)
Crone v. United States, 411 F. 2d 251 (5th Cir. 1969) . . . 38, 39 (90)
Croom v. State, 85 Ga. 718, 723, 724, 11 S.E. 1035, 1037 (1890) . . . 10, 16 (31), 17 (36)
Cupp v. Murphy, 412 U.S. 291, 294, 93 S. Ct. 2000, 2003 (1973) . . . 30, 31 (84)

—D—

Daily v. State, 136 Ga. App. 866, 222 S.E. 2d 682 (1975) . . . 47 (13)
Daniels v. State, 78 Ga. 98 (1866) . . . 106 (97)
Davidson v. State, 125 Ga. App. 502, 505, 188 S.E. 2d 124 (1972) . . . 50, 52 (92)
Davis v. Mississippi, 394 U.S. 721, 724, 727 (1969) . . . 27, 30, 31 (84)
Davis v. State, 79 Ga. 767, 768-69, 4 S.E. 318 (1887) . . . 72, 75 (16), 11 (36)
Davis v. State, 155 Ga. App. 511, 271 S.E. 2d 648 (1980) . . . 38 (11)
Delegal v. State, 109 Ga. 518, 521-22, 35 S.E. 105, 106 (1900) . . . 5 (30), 15 (31)
Denson v. State, 128 Ga. App. 456, 197 S.E. 2d 156 (1973) . . . 84, 85, 90, 92 (95), 98 (96)
Desist v. United States, 394 U.S. 244 (1969) . . . 7 (105)

Dickson v. State, 62 Ga. 583 (1879) . . . 53 (13)
Dickson v. State, 124 Ga. App. 406, 184 S.E. 2d 37 (1971) . . . 46 (91)
Dixon v. State, 12 Ga. App. 17, 18, 76 S.E. 794, 795 (1912) . . . 24 (37), 53 (39)
Douglass v. State, 152 Ga. 379, 391-92, 110 S.E. 168, 174 (1921) . . . 28, 29 (23), 10 (36)
Dover v. State, 109 Ga. 485, 488, 34 S.E. 1030, 1031 (1900) . . . 31 (37)
Draper v. United States, 358 U.S. 307 (1958) . . . 41 (12), 49 (13), 46 (64)
Dresch v. State, 125 Ga. App. 110, 186 S.E. 2d 496, 498 (1971) . . . 33 (62)
Dukes v. State, 109 Ga. App. 825, 826, 137 S.E. 2d 532, 534 (1964) . . . 28, 30 (45)
Dye v. State, 114 Ga. App. 299, 151 S.E. 2d 164 (1966) . . . 77 (16)
Dyke v. Taylor Impl. Mfg. Co., Inc., 391 U.S. 216 (1968) . . . 28 (74)

—E—

Eaker v. State, 4 Ga. App. 649, 652, 62 S.E. 99, 100-101 (1908) . . . 20 (21)
Earl v. State, 124 Ga. 28, 29, 52 S.E. 78, 79 (1905) . . . 41 (24)
Eaton v. State, 83 Ga. App. 82, 85, 62 S.E. 2d 677, 679 (1950) . . . 29 (37)
Elder v. Camp, 193 Ga. 320, 322-23, 18 S.E. 2d 622, 625 (1942) . . . 12 (51)

—F—

Faulkner v. State, 166 Ga. 645, 663, 144 S.E. 193, 201 (1928) . . . 54 (39)
Flournoy v. State, 205 S.E. 2d 473 (1974) . . . 27 (89)
Fomby v. State, 120 Ga. App. 387, 170 S.E. 2d 585, 586 (1969) . . . 12 (8), 13 (9), 19, 20 (61), 100 (97)
Forchard v. State, 130 Ga. App. 801, 204 S.E. 2d 516 (1974) . . . 3 (30)
Fowler v. State, 121 Ga. App. 22, 172 S.E. 2d 447 (1970) . . . 49, 51 (64), 6 (109)
Fowler v. State, 128 Ga. App. 501, 502, 197 S.E. 2d 502, 503 (1973) . . . 21 (61)
Franklin v. Anderson, 118 Ga. 860, 861-62, 863, 45 S.E. 698, 699, 700 (1903) . . . 4 (20), 16, 18, 19 (36)
French v. State, 99 Ga. App. 149, 152, 107 S.E. 2d 890, 894 (1959) . . . 22 (45)

—G—

Garner v. State, 124 Ga. App. 33, 35, 182 S.E. 2d 902, 904-05 (1971) . . . 14 (60), 17 (61), 15 (88)
Garner v. State, 154 Ga. App. 101, 267 S.E. 2d 813 (1980) . . . 2 (43)
Garrison v. State, 122 Ga. App. 757, 758, 178 S.E. 2d 744, 746 (1970) . . . 15 (72)
Geiger v. State, 129 Ga. App. 488, 492, 199 S.E. 2d 861, 864 (1973) . . .

46 (64)
Giddens v. State, 152 Ga. 195, 198-99, 108 S.E. 788, 790 (1921) . . . 26 (22)
Giddens v. State, 154 Ga. 54, 60-61, 113 S.E. 386, 389 (1922) . . . 2, 4 (35)
Giordenello v. United States, 357 U.S. 480, 486 (1958) . . . 33, 37 (11), 32 (62)
Goldman v. United States, 316 U.S. 129 (1942) . . . 2, 3 (104), 5 (105)
Goldstein v. United States, 316 U.S. 114 (1941) . . . 28 (89)
Gondor v. State, 129 Ga. App. 665, 200 S.E. 2d 477 (1973) . . . 11, 12 (88)
Goodwin v. Allen, 89 Ga. App. 187, 189, 78 S.E. 2d 804, 807 (1953) . . . 7 (20)
Graham v. State, 143 Ga. 440, 444-45, 446, 85 S.E. 328, 330, 331 (1915) . . . 14 (31), 9, 15 (36), 57 (39)
Grantling v. State, 229 Ga. 746, 194 S.E. 2d 405 (1972) . . . 29 (89)
Green v. State, 49 Ga. App. 252, 255, 175 S.E. 2d 28 (1934) . . . 65 (15)
Green v. State, 127 Ga. App. 713, 194 S.E. 2d 678 (1972) . . . 80 (94)
Green v. State, 250 Ga. 610, 299 S.E. 2d 544 (1983) . . . 20 (107)
Grimes v. United States, 405 F. 2d 477 (5th Cir. 1968) . . . 13 (88), 72 (93)
Groves v. State, 175 Ga. 37, 41, 164 S.E. 822, 824 (1932) . . . 35 (38)
Guest v. State, 230 Ga. 569, 198 S.E. 2d 158 (1973) . . . 22 (89)
Gustafson v. Florida, 414 U.S. 260 (1973) . . . 30, 33 (90), 48 (91)

—H—

Habersham v. State, 56 Ga. 62 (1876) . . . 12 (31)
Hansen v. State, 168 Ga. App. 304, 308 S.E. 2d 236 (1983) . . . 91 (95)
Hardin v. State, 203 Ga. 641, 645, 47 S.E. 2d 745, 747 (1948) . . . 54 (13)
Harper v. State, 129 Ga. 770, 59 S.E. 792 (1907) . . . 9 (31)
Harrell v. State, 75 Ga. 842, 846 (1885) . . . 40, 42 (38)
Harris v. State, 128 Ga. App. 22, 195 S.E. 2d 262 (1973) . . . 36 (23)
Harris v. United States, 390 U.S. 234, 236 (1968) . . . 17, 18 (72), 24 (84), 82 (94)
Hart v. United States, 316 F. 2d 916 (5th Cir. 1963) . . . 47 (91)
Hawkins v. State, 165 Ga. App. 278, 300 S.E. 2d 224 (1983) . . . 69, 70, 71, 72 (66)
Henry v. United States, 361 U.S. 98, 102 (1959) . . . 33 (23), 14 (88)
Hightower v. State, 228 Ga. 301, 185 S.E. 2d 82 (1971) . . . 7 (71)
Hines v. Adams, 27 Ga. App. 157, 158, 107 S.E. 618, 619 (1921) . . . 2 (3)
Hoffa v. United States, 385 U.S. 293, 302 (1966) . . . 17 (106)
Hogan v. Atkins, 411 F. 2d 576 (5th Cir. 1969) . . . 57 (92)
Holmes v. State, 5 Ga. App. 166, 169, 62 S.E. 716, 717-18 (1908) . . . 18 (21), 28 (37), 52, 56 (39)
Holtzendorf v. State, 125 Ga. App. 747, 750, 188 S.E. 2d 879, 881 . . . 10 (4), 7 (82)

Hood v. State, 229 Ga. 435, 192 S.E. 2d 154 (1972) . . . 46 (91)
Hunter v. State, 127 Ga. App. 664, 194 S.E. 2d 680 (1972) . . . 37 (90), 74 (93)
Husty v. United States, 282 U.S. 694 (1931) . . . 5, 8 (88)
Hutchins v. State, 3 Ga. App. 300, 59 S.E. 848 (1907) . . . 106 (97)

—J—

Jackson v. State, 34 Ga. App. 519, 130 S.E. 360 (1925) . . . 57 (14)
James v. Louisiana, 382 U.S. 36, 37 (1965) . . . 1, 2 (78)
J.C. Penney Co. v. Green, 108 Ga. App. 155, 157, 132 S.E. 2d 83, 85 (1963) . . . 57 (14)
Johnson v. Jackson, 140 Ga. App. 252, 230 S.E. 2d 756 (1976) . . . 3 (30), 8, 11 (31)
Johnson v. State, 111 Ga. App. 298, 306, 141 S.E. 2d 574, 581 (1965) . . . 41 (12), 33 (23)
Johnson v. State, 126 Ga. App. 93, 94, 189 S.E. 2d 900 (1972) . . . 5 (88)
Johnston v. State, 227 Ga. 387, 181 S.E. 2d 42 (1971) . . . 49 (13)
Joiner v. State, 66 Ga. App. 106, 17 S.E. 2d 101 (1941) . . . 9 (44)
Jones v. State, 114 Ga. 73, 74, 39 S.E. 861 (1901) . . . 4, 5 (35), 11, 13 (36)
Jones v. State, 126 Ga. App. 841, 843, 192 S.E. 2d 171, 173 (1972) . . . 11 (4), 1 (81)
Jones v. State, 127 Ga. App. 137, 193 S.E. 2d 38, 39 (1972) . . . 61, 62, (65)
Jones v. United States, 362 U.S. 257 (1960) . . . 39 (63), 68, 69 (93)

—K—

Katz v. United States, 389 U.S. 347, 351 (1967) . . . 2, 3, 6 (71), 16 (72), 1 (104)
Kelley v. State, 129 Ga. App. 131, 198 S.E. 2d 910 (1973) . . . 39, 44 (75), 14, 15 (83), 3 (87), 14, 15 (88), 43 (91), 9 (109)
Ker v. California, 374 U.S. 23, 42-43 (1962) . . . 17, 18 (72), 43 (75), 9 (80)

—L—

Lamb v. Dillard, 94 Ga. 206, 208, 21 S.E. 463, 464 (1894) . . . 34 (46)
L.B.B. v. State, 129 Ga. App. 163, 198 S.E. 2d 895, 896 (1973) . . . 6, 7 (82), 18 (89), 31 (90), 59 (92)
Lee v. United States, 343 U.S. 747 (1952) . . . 16 (106)
Lewis v. United States, 385 U.S. 206, 210 (1966) . . . 16 (72)
Lofton v. State, 122 Ga. App. 727, 178 S.E. 2d 693 (1970) . . . 55 (92)
Long v. State, 12 Ga. 293, 318 (1852) . . . 8, 13 (31)
Lopez v. United States, 373 U.S. 427 (1963) . . . 18 (106)
Lovett v. State, 111 Ga. App. 295, 141 S.E. 2d 595 (1965) . . . 10 (7),

15 (9), 52 (13)

Lowe v. Turner, 115 Ga. App. 503, 505, 154 S.E. 2d 792, 794 (1967) . . . 10 (7), 16, 19 (9), 52 (13)

—M—

Mapp v. Ohio, 367 U.S. 643 (1961) . . . 96 (96), 1 (108)

Marron v. United States, 275 U.S. 192 (1927) . . . 11 (60)

Marsh v. State, 223 Ga. 590, 157 S.E. 2d 273 (1967) . . . 29 (89)

Massey Stores, Inc. v. Reeves, 111 Ga. App. 227, 229, 141 S.E. 2d 227, 228 (1965) . . . 68 (15)

Maughon v. State, 7 Ga. App. 660, 666, 67 S.E. 842, 845 (1910) . . . 47, 48 (24)

McAllister v. State, 7 Ga. App. 541, 67 S.E. 221 (1910) . . . 26 (37)

McCain v. Bonner, 122 Ga. 842, 846, 51 S.E. 36, 38 (1905) . . . 59 (14)

McCray v. State, 134 Ga. 416, 426-27, 68 S.E. 62, 67 (1910) . . . 72, 73, 74 (16)

McDonald v. United States, 335 U.S. 451, 455 (1948) . . . 27 (73), 33, 34 (74)

McWilliams v. Interstate Bakeries, Inc., 439 F. 2d 16 (5th Cir. 1971) . . . 15 (31)

Merrill v. State, 130 Ga. App. 745, 204 S.E. 2d 632 (1974) . . . 27 (89)

Merritt v. State, 121 Ga. App. 832, 833, 175 S.E. 2d 890, 892 (1970) . . . 5 (109)

Messer v. State, 120 Ga. App. 747, 172 S.E. 2d 194 (1969), *cert. denied* 400 U.S. 866 (1970) . . . 13 (72)

Michelle v. State, 226 Ga. 450, 175 S.E. 2d 545 (1970) . . . 26, 27 (22)

Michigan v. Summers, 452 U.S. 692 (1980) . . . 65, 67, 68 (66)

Middlebrooks v. State, 135 Ga. App. 411, 218 S.E. 2d 110 (1975), *rev'd. on other grounds* 236 Ga. 52, 222 S.E. 2d 343 (1976) . . . 27 (45)

Miller v. United States, 357 U.S. 301 (1958) . . . 37 (38)

Mincey v. State, 251 Ga. 255, 261, 304 S.E. 2d 882, 888 (1983) . . . 36, 37 (38)

Miranda v. Arizona, 384 U.S. 436 (1966) . . . 1 (42)

Mitchell v. State, 126 Ga. 84, 54 S.E. 931 (1906) . . . 10 (44)

Mobley v. State, 130 Ga. App. 80, 202 S.E. 2d 465 (1973) . . . 21 (73), 10 (109)

Moody v. State, 120 Ga. 868, 869, 48 S.E. 340, 341 (1904) . . . 23, 24 (37)

Moon v. State, 120 Ga. App. 141, 169 S.E. 2d 632-36 (1969) . . . 12 (60), 106 (97)

Montgomery v. State, 155 Ga. App. 423, 270 S.E. 2d 825 (1980) . . . 15 (72)

Morrison v. State, 129 Ga. App. 558, 200 S.E. 2d 286 (1973) . . . 22 (89), 83 (94)

Morton v. State, 190 Ga. 792, 799, 10 S.E. 2d 836, 840, 841 (1940) . . .

10 (36), 20 (37)
Moses v. State, 6 Ga. App. 251, 253, 64 S.E. 699 (1906) . . . 18 (44)
Mullis v. State, 196 Ga. 569, 576, 577-78, 27 S.E. 2d 91, 97, 98 (1943) . . . 6 (20), 21, 30 (37), 58 (39)

—N—

Napper v. State, 200 Ga. 626, 629, 38 S.E. 2d 269, 271 (1946) . . . 18 (21), 22 (22), 22 (37), 51, 55 (39)
Newcomb v. United States, 327 F. 2d 649 (1964) . . . 42 (12)
Newkirk v. State, 57 Ga. App. 803, 807, 196 S.E. 911, 913 (1938) . . . 67 (15), 55 (64)
Newsome v. Scott, 151 Ga. 639, 107 S.E. 854 (1921) . . . 31 (45)
New York v. Belton, 453 U.S. 454 (1980) . . . 36 (90)
Nicholson v. United States, 355 F. 2d 80 (5th Cir. 1966), *cert denied* 384 U.S. 974 (1966) . . . 56 (92)
Nobles v. State, 81 Ga. App. 229, 58 S.E. 2d 496 (1950) . . . 9 (44)
Novak v. State, 130 Ga. App. 780, 204 S.E. 2d 491 (1974) . . . 8 (21), 3 (30)

—O—

Ocean S.S. Co. v. Williams, 69 Ga. 251, 262-63 (1882) . . . 26 (33)
Olmstead v. United States, 277 U.S. 438 (1928) . . . 2, 3, 4 (104)
On Lee v. United States, 343 U.S. 747 (1952) *rev'd. on other grounds* . . . 16 (106)
Ormond v. Ball, 120 Ga. 916, 921, 923-25, 48 S.E. 383, 385, 386-87 (1904) . . . 27 (10), 64, 67 (15), 85 (17), 55 (64)

—P—

Paige v. Potts, 354 F. 2d 212, 213-14 (1956) . . . 35 (23)
Paige v. State, 219 Ga. 569, 572, 134 S.E. 2d 793, 796 (1964) . . . 1 (108)
Papachristou v. City of Jacksonville, 405 U.S. 156 (1972) . . . 50 (92)
Patterson v. State, 126 Ga. App. 753, 191 S.E. 2d 584 (1972) . . . 32 (62)
Payton v. New York, 445 U.S. 573, 576 (1980) . . . 34 (38)
Pennaman v. Walton, 220 Ga. 295, 297-98, 138 S.E. 2d 571, 572-73 (1964) . . . 24 (45)
Phelps v. State, 106 Ga. App. 132, 126 S.E. 2d 429, 430 (1962) . . . 14 (21)
Phillips v. State, 66 Ga. 755 (1881) . . . 81 (16), 47 (38)
Pickett v. State, 99 Ga. 12, 15, 25 S.E. 608, 609 (1896) . . . 13 (21)
Piedmont Hotel Co. v. Henderson, 9 Ga. App. 672, 680, 681, 682, 72 S.E. 51, 55, 56 (1911) . . . 5 (20), 8 (21), 3 (30), 20 (44)
Pistor v. State, 219 Ga. 161, 165, 132 S.E. 2d 183, 185 (1963) . . . 35, 36 (23)
Porter v. State, 124 Ga. 297, 299, 302, 52 S.E. 283, 284, 285 (1905) . . .

Table of cases / 121

1 (6), 16 (51)
Preston v. United States, 376 U.S. 364 (1964) . . . 1 (87), 37 (90)

—R—

Raif v. State, 109 Ga. App. 354, 357, 358, 136 S.E. 2d 169, 172 (1964) . . . 34, 36, 38 (23)
Ramsey v. State, 92 Ga. 53, 63-64, 17 S.E. 613, 615 (1893) . . . 10 (21), 20 (37), 50 (39)
Redd v. Decker, 447 F. 2d 1346 (5th Cir. 1971) . . . 28, 29 (84)
Reece v. State, 152 Ga. App. 760, 264 S.E. 2d 258 (1979) . . . 39 (63)
Reed v. State, 126 Ga. App. 323, 190 S.E. 2d 587 (1972) . . . 18 (61), 100 (97), 101, 102 (97)
Reed v. State, 195 Ga. 842, 849-50, 25 S.E. 2d 692, 697 (1943) . . . 40 (23), 41 (24)
Register v. State, 124 Ga. App. 136, 183 S.E. 2d 68 (1971) . . . 42 (63)
Reid v. State, 129 Ga. App. 660, 200 S.E. 2d 456 (1973) . . . 35 (62)
Richardson v. State, 113 Ga. App. 163, 147 S.E. 2d 653, 654 (1966) . . . 37 (23)
Roach v. State, 221 Ga. 783, 147 S.E. 2d 299 (1966) . . . 32 (90)
Robinson v. State, 93 Ga. 77, 83-85, 88, 89, 18 S.E. 1018, 1019, 1020 (1893) . . . 17 (32), 8, 12, 13, 14 (36), 43, 45, 46 (38), 49 (39)
Rochin v. California, 342 U.S. 165 (1952) . . . 19 (83)
Ronemous v. State, 87 Ga. App. 588, 591, 74 S.E. 2d 676, 678 (1953) . . . 12 (21)
Rowland v. State, 117 Ga. App. 577, 161 S.E. 2d 422 (1968) . . . 35 (90), 44, 45 (91)
Rugendorf v. United States, 376 U.S. 528 (1964) . . . 42 (63)

—S—

Sams v. State, 121 Ga. App. 46, 172 S.E. 2d 473 (1970) . . . 40 (63)
Savannah News-Press, Inc. v. Harley, 100 Ga. App. 387, 388-89, 391, 111 S.E. 2d 259, 263, 264 (1959) . . . 17 (9), 4 (20), 30 (23), 27 (37), 4 (43)
Scher v. United States, 305 U.S. 251 (1938) . . . 5, 9 (88)
Schmerber v. California, 384 U.S. 757 (1966) . . . 18 (83)
Schneckloth v. Bustamonte, 412 U.S. 218 (1973) . . . 10 (72)
Scull v. State, 122 Ga. App. 696, 178 S.E. 2d 270 (1970) . . . 61, 63, 64 (65)
Segars v. Cornwell, 128 Ga. App. 245, 196 S.E. 2d 341 (1973) . . . 57 (14)
Sgro v. United States, 287 U.S. 206 (1932) . . . 50 (64)
Shafer v. State, 192 Ga. 748, 754-55, 20 S.E. 2d 34, 38 (1943) . . . 11 (21)
Shearer v. State, 128 Ga. App. 809, 198 S.E. 2d 369 (1973) . . . 46 (91)
Shipley v. California, 395 U.S. 818, 820 (1969) . . . 1 (78)
Shirley v. City of College Park, 102 Ga. App. 10, 115 S.E. 2d 469, 470 (1960) . . . 21 (21), 54 (25), 10 (51)

Sibron v. New York, 392 U.S. 41, 62 (1968) . . . 12 (4)
Silverman v. United States, 365 U.S. 505 (1961) . . . 6 (105)
Smith v. State, 84 Ga. App. 79, 82, 65 S.E. 2d 709, 711 (1951) . . . 2 (6), 1 (20)
Snelling v. State, 87 Ga. 50, 13 S.E. 154 (1891) . . . 16 (31), 38 (38)
Southern Ry. v. Gresham, 114 Ga. 183, 184, 39 S.E. 883 (1901) . . . 6 (30)
Spinelli v. United States, 393 U.S. 410 (1969) . . . 49 (13), 40 (63)
Stacey v. Emery, 97 U.S. 642, 645 (1878) . . . (34) 11
Stalling v. Splain, 253 U.S. 339 (1920) . . . 76 (27)
Stanley v. Georgia, 394 U.S. 557, 571 (1969) . . . 79 (67)
Stanley v. State, 224 Ga. 259, 161 S.E. 2d 309 (1968) . . . 78 (67)
State v. Middlebrooks, 236 Ga. 52, 222 S.E. 2d 343 (1976) . . . 8 (44)
State v. Swift, 232 Ga. 535, 207 S.E. 2d 459 (1974) . . . 62 (92), 64, 65 (93)
State v. Watts, 154 Ga. App. 789, 270 S.E. 2d 52 (1980) . . . 41 (63)
State v. Whittle, 37 S.E. 923 (S.C. 1901) . . . 72 (26)
Steele v. State, 118 Ga. App. 433, 434, 164 S.E. 2d 255, 256 (1968) . . . 100 (97)
Steele v. United States, 267 U.S. 498, 503 (1925) . . . 10 (60), 100 (97)
Stone v. National Surety Corp., 57 Ga. App. 427, 195 S.E. 905 (1938) . . . 19 (44), 29 (45)
Stoner v. California, 376 U.S. 483 (1964) . . . 12 (72)
Strauss v. Stynchcombe, 224 Ga. 859, 165 S.E. 2d 302, 306 (1968) . . . 47 (64)
Strickland v. State, 226 Ga. 750, 177 S.E. 2d 238 (1970) . . . 25, 29 (89)
Swift v. State, 131 Ga. App. 231, 206 S.E. 2d 51 (1974) . . . 60, 62 (92)

—T—

Tanner v. State, 114 Ga. App. 35, 150 S.E. 2d 189 (1966) . . . 22 (89)
Tarver v. State, 90 Tenn. 485, 16 S.W. 1041 (1891) . . . 71 (26)
Tennessee v. Garner, 105 S. Ct. 1584 (1985) . . . 32 (37)
Terry v. Ohio, 392 U.S. 1, 22, 24, 26-27 (1968) . . . 7 (3), 8 (4), 1, 2 (81), 5, 8, 9, 11 (82), 31 (90), 50 (92)
Thomas v. State, 91 Ga. 204, 206, 207, 18 S.E. 305, 306 (1892) . . . 2 (6), 1 (20), 39 (23), 57 (39)
Thompson v. State, 230 Ga. 610, 198 S.E. 2d 288 (1973) . . . 109 (97)
Thornton v. State, 125 Ga. App. 374, 187 S.E. 2d 583 (1972) . . . 43 (63)
Thrall v. State, 122 Ga. App. 427, 177 S.E. 2d 192 (1970) . . . 22 (61)
Tolbert v. Hicks, 158 Ga. App. 642, 281 S.E. 2d 368 (1981) . . . 4 (3)
Tolbert v. State, 224 Ga. 291, 161 S.E. 2d 279 (1968) . . . 14 (72)
Traylor v. State, 127 Ga. App. 409, 193 S.E. 2d 876 (1972) . . . 24 (89), 42 (91)
Turner v. McGee, 217 Ga. 769, 773, 125 S.E. 2d 36, 39 (1962) . . . 6 (49)

–U–

United States, v. Altizer, 477 F. 2d 846 (5th Cir. 1973) . . . 41 (90)
United States v. Baty, 486 F. 2d 240 (5th Cir. 1973) . . . 46 (91)
United States v. Boyd, 436 F. 2d 1203 (1971) . . . 25 (84)
United States v. Brown, 411 F. 2d 478 (5th Cir. 1969) . . . 5, 11 (88)
United States v. Colbert, 474 F. 2d 174, 186 (5th Cir. 1973) . . . 78 (93)
United States v. Di Re, 332 U.S. 581 (1948) . . . 104 (97)
United States v. Edwards, 441 F. 2d 745, 749, 752, 753 (5th Cir. 1971) . . . 66, 69, 71, 79 (93), 82 (94)
United States v. Edwards, 415 U.S. 800 (1974) . . . 44 (75), 17 (83)
United States v. Ferrone, 438 F. 2d 381 (3rd Cir. 1971) . . . 20 (61)
United States v. Fike, 449 F. 2d 191 (5th Cir. 1971) . . . 22 (89)
United States v. Five Gambling Devices, 119 F. Supp. 641 (D.C. Ga. 1952) . . . 18 (110)
United States v. Gravitt, 484 F. 2d 375, 378 (5th Cir. 1973) . . . 24, 25 (84), 89, 92 (95), 95, 97 (96)
United States v. Gulledge, 469 F. 2d 713 (5th Cir. 1972) . . . 76 (93)
United States v. Harris, 403 U.S. 573 (1971) . . . 45 (64)
United States v. Hill, 442 F. 2d 259 (5th Cir. 1971) . . . 8 (88)
United States v. Jackson, 451 F. 2d 259 (5th Cir. 1971) . . . 28, 29 (84)
United States v. Jones, 352 F. Supp. 369 (S.D. Ga. 1972) . . . 3 (3)
United States v. Kelehar, 470 F. 2d 176 (5th Cir. 1972) . . . 82 (94), 92 (95), 94 (96)
United States v. Lee, 274 U.S. 559, 563 (1927) . . . 16 (72), 20 (73)
United States v. Lipscomb, 435 F. 2d 780, 795 (5th Cir. 1970) . . . 24, 25 (84)
United States v. Maryland, 479 F. 2d 566 (5th Cir. 1973) . . . 75 (93)
United States v. Newsome, 432 F. 2d 51 (5th Cir. 1970) . . . 35 (90)
United States v. Robinson, 414 U.S. 218 (1973) . . . 12, 16 (83), 30, 33 (90), 48 (91)
United States v. Ross, 456 U.S. 798 (1982) . . . 16 (88), 17 (89)
United States v. United States District Court, 407 U.S. 297 (1972) . . . 4 (71)
United States v. Ventresca, 380 U.S. 102, 105-6, 108-9 (1969) . . . 43, 44, 45, 46 (12), 38, 44 (63), 48 (64), 1 (71), 69 (93)
United States v. Williams, 230 F. Supp. 47, 51 (1961), *aff'd* 314 F. 2d 795 (6th Cir. 1963) . . . 70 (26)
United States v. Willis, 85 F. Supp. 745 (S.D. Cal. 1949) . . . 20 (83)

–V–

Veasey v. State, 113 Ga. App. 187, 147 S.E. 2d 515 (1966) . . . 58 (65)

—W—

Wadley v. McCommon, 154 Ga. 420, 114 S.E. 357 (1922) . . . 28 (10)

Walker v. State, 220 Ga. 415, 419-20, 139 S.E. 2d 278, 282 (1964), *rev'd on other grounds* 381 U.S. 355 (1965) . . . 3 (6), 5 (57)

Walker v. State, 46 Ga. App. 824, 828, 169 S.E. 315, 317 (1933) . . . 6 (30), 12 (31)

Walker v. State, 144 Ga. App. 838, 242 S.E. 2d 753 (1978) . . . 4 (30)

Wallace v. State, 131 Ga. App. 204, 205 S.E. 2d 523 (1974) . . . 68 (66)

Warden v. Hayden, 387 U.S. 294 (1967) . . . 64 (25), 26 (73), 30, 31, 37 (74), 6, 7, 8 (79), 10 (80)

Washington v. Chrisman, 454 U.S. 1 (1981) . . . 42 (75)

Whisman v. State, 223 Ga. 124, 153 S.E. 2d 548 (1967) . . . 25 (45)

White v. United States, 401 U.S. 745, 749 (1971) . . . 16, 17 (106)

Whitfield v. State, 115 Ga. App. 231, 232, 154 S.E. 2d 294, 296 (1967) . . . 21 (45)

Whitlock v. State, 124 Ga. App. 599, 185 S.E. 2d 90 (1971) . . . 71 (93), 81 (94)

Wiggins v. State, 14 Ga. App. 314, 315, 80 S.E. 724 (1914) . . . 43 (24)

Williams v. Sewell, 121 Ga. 665, 49 S.E. 732 (1905) . . . 25 (10)

Williams v. State, 148 Ga. 310, 96 S.E. 385 (1918) . . . 53 (39)

Williams v. State, 129 Ga. App. 103, 105, 198 S.E. 2d 683 (1973) . . . 22 (73), 5 (88), 58 (92)

Williamson v. United States, 207 U.S. 425, 444-46, (1908) . . . 3 (48)

Williford v. State, 121 Ga. 173, 176-77, 48 S.E. 962, 964 (1904) . . . 46 (24)

Willis v. State, 122 Ga. App. 455, 177 S.E. 2d 487 (1970) . . . 99 (96)

Wilson v. State, 223 Ga. 531, 156 S.E. 2d 446 (1967) . . . 7 (20)

Windsor v. State, 122 Ga. App. 767, 178 S.E. 2d 751 (1970) . . . 52 (64)

Wolf v. Colorado, 338 U.S. 25, 27-28 (1949) . . . 1 (57)

Wood v. State, 118 Ga. App. 477, 164 S.E. 2d 233 (1968) . . . 50 (64)

Wood v. State, 224 Ga. 121, 160 S.E. 2d 368 (1968) . . . 103, 105 (97)

Wright v. State, 12 Ga. App. 514, 77 S.E. 657 (1913) . . . 13 (60), 107 (97)

—Y—

Yancy v. Fidelity Casualty Co. of New York, 96 Ga. App. 476, 478-80, 100 S.E. 2d 653, 655-56 (1957) . . . 41, 44 (24)

Yates v. State, 127 Ga. 813, 818, 819-20, 56 S.E. 1017, 1019, 1020, (1907) . . . 42, 45 (24)

Ybarra v. Illinois, 444 U.S. 85, 93 (1979) . . . 66 (66)

Young v. State, 113 Ga. App. 497, 148 S.E. 2d 461 (1966) . . . 8 (71), 23, 26 (89)

—Z—

Zap v. United States, 328 U.S. 624 (1946) . . . 5 (71), 22 (89)

Table of Statutes

Note: The numbers following each statute refer to the footnote and page numbers. The first number(s) indicates the footnote number of the specific statute. The number enclosed in parentheses is the page number of the text on which the statute is discussed.

Code of Alabama

15-10-7 (1975) . . . 73 (26)

Florida Statutes Annotated

941.31 (1968) . . . 69 (26)

General Statutes of North Carolina

15A-404 . . . 74 (26)

Official Code of Georgia Annotated

§5A-350 . . . 18 (52)
§6-30-20, 27 . . . 11, 15 (51)
§16-3-22 . . . 18 (32), 43, 48 (38)
§16-9-20 . . . 18 (9)
§16-10-52 . . . 49 (24)
§16-11-39 . . . 25 (37)
§16-11-60 . . . 20 (107)
§16-11-60 through 69 . . . 8 (105)
§16-11-62 . . . 10 (105)
§16-11-64 . . . 12 (106)
§16-11-64(b)(1) . . . 11 (105)
§16-11-64(b)(3) . . . 13 (106)
§16-11-64(b)(4) . . . 14 (106)
§16-11-66 . . . 15 (106)
§16-13-20 through 55 . . . 22 (53)
§16-13-70 through 76 . . . 23 (53)
§16-14-49 . . . 87 (95)
§17-2-1 . . . 56, 58, 59 (25)
§17-2-2 . . . 62 (25)
§17-2-3 . . . 61 (25), 75 (26)
§17-4-1 . . . 2, 5, 6 (3), 4 (49)
§17-4-2 . . . 5 (49)
§17-4-3 . . . 33 (38)
§17-4-20 . . . 2 (20), 48, 50 (24), 22 (32), 40 (75)
§17-4-21 . . . 13, 15 (44)

§17-4-23 . . . 15, 16, 17 (21), 61 (92)
§17-4-24 . . . 66 (15), 40, 41, 44 (38), 54 (64)
§17-4-25 . . . 79 (15), 86 (17), 14 (44), 13 (51)
§17-4-26 . . . 3 (42), 16, 17 (44)
§17-4-27 . . . 35 (46)
§17-4-40 . . . 20, 21 (9), 31 (10), 56 (14), 62 (15)
§17-4-41 . . . 7, 8, 9 (7), 50 (13)
§17-4-41.5 . . . 51 (13)
§17-4-42 . . . 84, 87, 88 (17)
§17-4-44 . . . 5(6), 79 (16), 63 (25)
§17-4-45 . . . 55 (13), 61 (14)
§17-4-46 . . . 11 (8)
§17-4-60 . . . 2 (30), 7, 9 (31)
§17-4-62 . . . 24 (32), 25, 27 (33), 26, 28 (45)
§17-4-70 . . . 4 (6)
§17-5-1 . . . 9 (4), 38 (74), 45, 46 (76), 3 (78), 4 (79), 30 (90), 88 (95)
§17-5-1(a)(4) . . . 25 (73)
§17-5-1(a)(5) . . . 24 (73)
§17-5-2 . . . 93 (95)
§17-5-20 . . . 23 (61)
§17-5-21 . . . 25 (61), 31 (62), 37 (63)
§17-5-21(a) . . . 73 (66)
§17-5-21(a)(1) . . . 75 (67)
§17-5-21(a)(5) . . . 74, 76 (67)
§17-5-22 . . . 6 (60), 27, 28, 36 (62)
§17-5-22(a) . . . 29 (62)
§17-5-23 . . . 4 (57), 8, 9 (60)
§17-5-24 . . . 7 (60), 53 (64)
§17-5-25 . . . 56 (65), 80 (67)
§17-5-26 . . . 57 (65), 8 (109)
§17-5-27 . . . 59, 60 (65)
§17-5-28 . . . 65 (66), 32 (90), 112 (98)
§17-5-29 . . . 81, 82, 83 (68)
§17-5-30 . . . 2 (108)
§17-5-30(a)(2) . . . 3 (108)
§17-5-31 . . . 4 (109)
§17-6-1 . . . 31, 32 (45)
§17-6-2 . . . 33 (46)
§17-6-16 . . . 6, 7 (44)
§17-7-20 . . . 11 (44), 26 (62)
§17-7-22 . . . 12 (44)
§17-8-29 . . . 84 (68)
§17-13-20 through 30 . . . 30 (10)

§17-13-22 . . . 77 (27)
§17-13-34 . . . 83 (16)
§19-13-1 . . . 3 (20), 23, 24 (22)
§20-3-72 . . . 29 (53)
§24-10-1 . . . 6 (49)
§25-2-9 . . . 25 (53)
§26-4-51 . . . 24 (53)
§27-3-45 . . . 87 (95)
§27-1-18 . . . 20 (52)
§27-3-2,3 . . . 87 (95)
§31-14-13 . . . 21 (32)
§35-2-32 . . . 3 (50)
§35-2-33 . . . 4, 5, 6, 7 (50)
§35-2-71 . . . 26 (53)
§35-3-4 . . . 8 (51)
§36-8-5 . . . 14 (51)
§36-32-3 . . . 12 (44)
§36-33-3 . . . 17(110)
§36-33-4 . . . 16 (110)
§37-1-21 . . . 28 (53)
§40-5-57 . . . 14 (4)
§40-6-391 . . . 23 (84)
§40-6-392 . . . 21, 22 (84)
§40-8-200 . . . 15 (4)
§42-5-35 . . . 19 (52)
§42-8-38 . . . 21 (52)
§42-9-48 . . . 29 (10)
§45-16-9 . . . 17 (51)
§45-16-35 . . . 24 (10)
§50-2-1 *et seq* . . . 60 (25)
§50-16-6 . . . 27 (53)
§51-7-1 . . . 39 (11), 1 (50)
§51-7-2 . . . 2 (50)
§51-7-3 . . . 40 (11)

Tennessee Code Annotated

40-7-203 (1982) . . . 68 (26)

United States Court of Appeals

18 U.S.C.A. §2510-20 (1970) . . . 9 (107)
18 U.S.C.A. §2520 (1970) . . . 15 (110)
42 U.S.C.A. §1983 (1970) . . . 11, 13 (110)

Glossary

Affidavit — A written or printed declaration or statement of facts, made voluntarily, confirmed by the oath or affirmation of the party making it, and sworn to be true by the maker before a person having authority to administer such oath or affirmation.

Arrest — The restraint, no matter how slight, of the liberty of a person to come and go as he or she pleases.

Arrest warrant — A judicial command to arrest a particular individual and to bring that person promptly before the magistrate issuing the warrant or before some other designated judicial officer.

Carroll rule — A rule of law, created by the U.S. Supreme Court, allowing officers to search movable vehicles when probable cause exists to believe that a crime has been or is being committed.

Curtilage — All of the buildings in close proximity to the dwelling identified in a search warrant that are used in connection with the dwelling for family purposes (e.g., garage, storehouse, tool shed, etc.).

Due process — The principle that the government must act in a fair and reasonable manner when it threatens to deprive individuals of life, liberty, or property. It is embodied in the Fifth, Sixth, and Fourteenth amendments to the U.S. Constitution.

Eavesdropping — Listening in to an otherwise private conversation. When done using electronic devices, the courts consider such eavesdropping a search and seizure. *See also* Investigative warrant.

Exigent circumstances — Those events or situations requiring immediate action and which make obtaining a warrant impractical.

Felony — A serious crime punishable by a prison sentence of a year or more. Examples are murder, kidnapping, armed robbery, arson, rape, or forgery.

Implied consent statute — When applied to motor vehicle law, this states that a police officer may request a breath test incident to a lawful arrest of a person whom the officer has reasonable cause to believe has been driving under the influence of alcohol or other intoxicating substance. The suspect may refuse such test but faces a six-month suspension of driver's license.

In the officer's presence — This means the same as "within the officer's immediate, personal knowledge" through the officer's seeing, hearing, or by use of any other of his or her senses.

Inventory search — A search of a vehicle belonging to a suspect in custody for purposes of protecting the owner's property and to safeguard the police from groundless claims for lost possessions. Such search may be of the entire vehicle, and all property found in the vehicle must be listed in an inventory.

Investigative stop or detention — Stopping a person for purposes of investigation under circumstances not amounting to an arrest. The person stopped is free to leave and may not be required to answer any questions asked by the investigating officer.

Investigative warrant — An electronic surveillance warrant. A document that gives police the authority to gain evidence in a criminal case using a wiretap or other eavesdropping methods.

John Doe warrant — A warrant issued for a specific person whose name is not known at the time the warrant is issued. In order to be valid, the warrant must describe the person to be arrested sufficiently to make identification of the person possible.

Miranda warning — A statement of the rights of a person in police custody. The reading of these rights, taken from the Fifth, Sixth, and Fourteenth amendments of the U.S. Constitution, to a suspect in custody is a necessary part of due process.

Misdemeanor — A crime less serious than a felony. A misdemeanor carries a maximum penalty of one year or less in jail and/or a fine of $1,000 or less. Examples are speeding and theft of less than $500.

Particularity requirement — A rule of law and the statutory requirement that the person and/or place to be arrested and/or searched be described with sufficient particularity on the face of the warrant to allow a prudent officer executing the warrant to be able to locate the person and/or place definitely and with reasonable certainty.

Plain view doctrine — Objects are seizable without a warrant or without being specified in a warrant when those objects, being in plain view, can be observed by an officer who does not have to disturb the scene to observe them. This does not constitute a search. (See important restrictions at p. 72.)

Posse comitatus — The citizens who are called either verbally or in writing to assist an officer.

Probable cause — A reasonable ground of suspicion, supported by circumstances sufficiently strong in themselves to warrant a cautious man in the belief that the party is guilty of the offense with which he or she is charged.

Reasonable suspicion — A belief or suspicion that is based on the officer's natural senses, experience, and good judgment.

Reasonable time — That time of day when a warrant is to be served, as yet undefined by the courts but usually during daylight hours.

Search warrant — A document issued by a judge which authorizes a police search at a specified location for a certain item and the seizure of that item. See Investigative warrant for seeking evidence through means of eavesdropping.

Stop and frisk — A two-step procedure in which an officer stops a person and searches that person by patting down the person's *outer* clothing or garments for a gun or a weapon. The officer must have reasonable suspicion that criminal activity might be afoot before making a stop and frisk.

Technical arrest — When an officer restrains a person's freedom to walk away with the intention of charging that person with an offense that would probably lead to prosecution.

Index

—A—

Abandoned vehicles . . . 93-94
Abusive language, use of by person arrested . . . 37
Accosting suspicious person as constituting arrest . . . 3
Accosting suspicious person as constituting investigative detention . . . 3-4
Activities in plain view . . . 72-73, 107, 109. *See also* Objects in plain view
Address of accused
   in warrant, as means of identifying person sought . . . 8
   records as containing . . . 46
Admissibility of illegally seized evidence . . . 108, 109
Advising accused of constitutional rights . . . 42, 43
Affidavit for arrest warrant
   clerk, taken by . . . 10, 15
   contents of, requirements as to . . . 13, 14
   error as invalidating . . . 13
   filed by peace officer . . . 9
   filed by private citizen . . . 9
   form of . . . 14
   hearsay, containing . . . 11
   inaccuracy as invalidating . . . 13
   informants' tips, based on . . . 12, 13
   oath in, necessity for . . . 14
   officials authorized to take . . . 15
   probable cause in, necessity for . . . 10, 11
   requirements for, compliance with . . . 13, 14
Affidavit for search warrant
   contents of, requirements as to . . . 63
   informants' tips, based on . . . 63-64
   particularity requirements for . . . 63
   probable cause, necessity for . . . 63-64
   sample copy . . . 58
Age of accused, records as containing . . . 46
Alcoholic beverages. *See* Intoxicating liquors
Ambassadors, immunity of . . . 48
Appearance of accused, describing in warrant . . . 8-9
Arrest
   requirements for lawful . . . 74-75
   search incident to, general . . . 74-76
   search of person incident to . . . 82-85
   search of premises incident to . . . 78-80
   search of vehicle incident to . . . 87, 90-91
   stopping train to . . . 38
   to prevent failure of justice . . . 22-23
   what constitutes . . . 3-4
   with warrant (Chapter 2)
   without warrant (Chapter 3)
   wrong person . . . 15
Articles which may be seized . . . 66-67
Assault, illegal arrest as . . . 39
Assistance
   fellow officer rendering . . . 38
   liability of person rendering . . . 32
   posse . . . 38-39
   private person rendering . . . 32, 38
   right to summon . . . 38
Attorney, right of accused to have . . . 42
Authority to arrest
   badge as showing . . . 36
   duty to make known . . . 36
   hospital staff as having . . . 32
   knowledge or notice of . . . 36
   out of state . . . 25-27
   private person as having . . . 30-32
   resistance to arrest in case of lack of . . . 36-37

134/ ARREST/SEARCH AND SEIZURE

territorial extent of, with warrant ... 16
territorial extent of, without warrant ... 25-27
uniform as showing ... 36
warrant, possession of as giving ... 35-36
Automobiles, search of (Chapter 13 generally). *See also* Motor vehicles
abandoned ... 93-94
carrying contraband ... 88-89
description of automobile in warrant ... 61
impounded ... 94-96
incident to arrest ... 90-91
incident to traffic violation ... 91-93
inventories ... 94-96
investigative stop, leading to ... 91-93
moving vehicles, suspected of carrying contraband ... 88-89
requiring search warrant for ... 96-98
roadblocks ... 92-93
stopped vehicles, as ... 89-93
within the curtilage ... 97-98
without a search warrant ... 88-96

—B—

Badge, authority to arrest as shown by ... 36
Bail
bondsman's right to arrest defaulter without warrant ... 32
bondsman not limited by state boundaries ... 32
officials authorized to accept ... 45-46
Beating person arrested ... 36-37
Blood tests ... 83-84
Body, search of. *See* Search of person
Breaking doors to execute warrant ... 38
Breath test ... 83-84
Buildings, search of. *See* Premises, search of

—C—

Campus police (UGA), jurisdiction of ... 53
Car, search of. *See* Automobile, search of
Carroll rule searches ... 87-89
Citizen's arrest. *See* Private person, arrest by
Citizens as posse members ... 38
City police, jurisdiction of ... 51
Civil action for illegal searches ... 110
Clerk of court
issuing warrant ... 10
taking affidavit ... 15
Commitment hearing
authority to hold ... 44
delay in holding ... 44, 45
for arrest made with warrant ... 44-45
for arrest made without warrant ... 45
officials authorized to hold ... 44
questioning legal or illegal arrest ... 44
time of holding ... 44, 45
waiver of ... 44
Concealed weapon, arrest for carrying ... 21
Conditional releasee, warrant for ... 10
Conduct of accused
delaying commitment hearing ... 45
preventing production of warrant ... 36
resisting arrest ... 36-37, 39
Confessions, advising accused of constitutional rights as affecting admissibility of ... 42
Confinement
as constituting arrest ... 3
as illegal arrest, *see* Illegal arrest
following citizen's arrest ... 33
prior to commitment hearing ... 44, 45
Congressmen, immunity of ... 48
Consent to arrest ... 3

Consent searches . . . 71-72, 89, 110
Constable . . .
  right to accept bail . . . 45-46
Constitutional rights, necessity of advising accused of . . . 42
Contemporaneous requirement . . . 75, 90
Contraband. *See* Evidence, seizure of
Contraband searches of vehicles . . . 88-89
Control over person arrested . . . 3
Coroner
  jurisdiction to arrest . . . 51
  warrant, authority to issue . . . 10
Correctional officer, authority of . . . 52
County police, jurisdiction of . . . 51
Courts. *See also* Commitment hearing
  issuing warrant . . . 9-10
  returning warrant before . . . 17
  "special warrant" . . . 17, 44
  taking accused before . . . 44, 45
  taking affidavit . . . 15
Curtilage, search of . . . 60, 97-98
Custodial arrest, search of person under . . . 83
Custody
  of person arrested . . . 3
  search . . . 83, 84, 94-96

—D—

Date of offense
  stating in affidavit . . . 13
  stating in warrant . . . 7
Deadly force, use of to prevent escape . . . 37, 65
Demanding admission before entering private premises . . . 38
Department of Human Resources institutional police . . . 53
Deputies
  authority of deputy clerk to take affidavit . . . 10
  possessing and producing of warrant . . . 35-36
  wardens', jurisdiction of . . . 52

Description of person sought in warrant . . . 8
John Doe . . . 9
  regarding officers' arrest of . . . 15
  ways of giving . . . 8
Designation of offense in warrant . . . 9
Detention
  as constituting arrest . . . 3
  place in later search . . . 75, 83
Driver's license, stopping vehicle for inspection of . . . 4, 91, 92
Drug inspectors, jurisdiction of . . . 52-53
Duress as invalidating waiver
  of commitment hearing . . . 44
  of constitutional rights . . . 42

—E—

Eavesdropping and wiretapping (*see* Chapter 14 generally)
Electronic surveillance (*see* Chapter 14 generally). *See also* Investigative warrant
Elements of offense, warrant as stating . . . 7
Entering the premises . . . 65
  during darkness . . . 38
  private, entering to arrest . . . 38
Escape
  arrest by private person during . . . 31
  arrest of fugitives . . . 24
  arrest to prevent . . . 21-22
  force, use of to prevent . . . 37
  rearrest after . . . 24
  shooting or killing to prevent . . . 37
Evidence
  advising accused of constitutional rights as affecting admissibility of . . . 42
  as information from others, arrest without warrant on basis of . . . 12-13, 21
  holding person for investigation in order to obtain . . . 23

seizure of, illegal . . . 108-9
seizure of, legal . . . 66-67, 72-76
Exclusionary rule . . . 108-9
Executive security guards, jurisdiction of . . . 53
Exigent circumstances search . . . 73-74
Extradition, validity of warrant in . . . 16

–F–

False imprisonment, delay of commitment hearing as constituting . . . 44, 45
Felony
   arrest to prevent . . . 23
   committed in presence of officer . . . 20-21
   force allowed during arrest . . . 36-37, 39
   private person, arrest by . . . 30-31, 32
   resistance during arrest for . . . 36-39
   shooting or killing . . . 37
   warrant, arrest without . . . 20, 23
Fingerprints . . . 84
Fire marshal, jurisdiction of . . . 53
Fresh pursuit. *See* Hot pursuit
Force and resistance
   duty to submit to lawful arrest . . . 39
   excessive force . . . 36-37, 39
   forcible entry . . . 38, 65
   resistance, when justified . . . 36, 39
   self-defense . . . 36-37
   shooting or killing . . . 37
Forcible entry . . . 38, 65
Foreign ministers, immunity of . . . 48
Frisk . . . 4, 81-82
Fugitives
   arrest of . . . 16, 24, 50
   from other states . . . 10, 16
   rearrest . . . 24

–G–

General Assembly, immunity of members . . . 48-49

Good faith as not justifying arrest . . . 23

–H–

Hearings. *See* Commitment hearing
Hearsay
   affidavit containing . . . 11
   as basis for search warrant . . . 63
Homicide
   in making arrest . . . 37
   in resistance to arrest . . . 37
Hot pursuit . . . 25-26, 74, 79-80
   across state line . . . 25-26
House of Representatives, immunity of members . . . 48
Houses. *See* Premises, search of

–I–

Identity
   designation of person sought in warrant . . . 8
   in affidavit . . . 13
   in warrant . . . 7
   of larceny victim . . . 13
   of person arrested, necessity for correct . . . 15
   officer's duty to reveal . . . 36
   when two persons have same name . . . 15
   when wrong person is arrested . . . 15
Illegal arrest
   assault by officer . . . 37, 39
   delay in making arrest . . . 23-24
   resistance to . . . 39
   wrong person . . . 15
Illegally seized evidence. *See* Evidence, seizure of
Immunity from arrest
   ambassadors . . . 48
   Congress, members of . . . 48
   General Assembly, members of . . . 48-49
   militia, members of . . . 49
   ministers, foreign . . . 48
   witnesses . . . 49
Impounded vehicles . . . 94-96

Index / 137

Informants' tips
  affidavit, requirements as to ... 12-13
  as basis for search warrant ... 63
  corroboration, necessity for ... 13
  credibility, requirements as to ... 12-13
  probable cause for arrest ... 12-13
Information of others
  arrest without warrant based on ... 21
  oath, necessity for affidavit ... 14
Interrogation, necessity of advising accused of constitutional rights before ... 42
Intoxicating liquors
  arrest for violation of law regarding ... 51-52, 84
  care of property of prisoner under the influence ... 42-43
  offense committed in officer's presence ... 20-21
Inventory of articles seized ... 68
Inventory searches
  automobiles ... 94-96
  person ... 84
Investigatory stop of vehicle, searches incident to ... 91-93
Investigative warrant ... 105-7
Investigation, holding suspect for purposes of ... 23

—J—

Janitors and guards of public buildings, jurisdiction of ... 53
John Doe warrant ... 9, 61
Judges
  affidavit, authority to take ... 15
  commitment hearing, authority to hold ... 44
  granting "special warrants" ... 17, 44
  returning warrant before ... 17
  taking accused before ... 44, 45
  warrant, authority to issue ... 9-10
Jurisdiction
  city police ... 51
  conservation rangers ... 52
  coroners ... 51
  county police ... 51
  Department of Human Resources institutional police ... 53
  drug inspectors ... 52-53
  executive security guards ... 53
  fire marshal ... 53
  Georgia Bureau of Investigation ... 51
  Georgia State Patrol ... 50
  janitors and guards of public buildings ... 53
  marshals ... 51
  prison guards, wardens, and correctional officers ... 52
  probation officers ... 52
  revenue agents ... 51-52
  sheriffs ... 51
  University System of Georgia campus police ... 54

—L—

Landlord and tenant consent ... 72
Larceny
  affidavit requirements when charged ... 13
  warrant requirements when charged ... 7
Lawful arrest requirements ... 75
Lawyer, right of accused to have ... 42
Liability of police officers
  for illegal search ... 109-10
  upon making warrantless arrest ... 50

—M—

Malicious arrest ... 11, 50
Militia, immunity of members ... 49
Misdemeanor
  committed in presence of officer ... 20-21
  force allowed during arrest ... 36-37
  private person, arrest by ... 30
  resistance to arrest for ... 37

138 / ARREST/SEARCH AND SEIZURE

shooting or killing . . . 37
warrant, arrest without . . . 20-21
Mistake
   in affidavit, effect of . . . 13
   in arrest of private person for misdemeanor not actually committed . . . 30
   in arrest of wrong person . . . 15
Mistreating person arrested . . . 37
Mobility doctrine. See Carroll rule searches
Motion to suppress evidence (see Chapter 15 generally)
   exclusionary rule . . . 108-9
   grounds for suppression . . . 108-9
Motor vehicles
   arrest to prevent escape in . . . 21
   Georgia State Patrol . . . 50
   search of, incident to arrest . . . 90-91
   stopping as constituting arrest . . . 4
   stopping to check for compliance with safety standards . . . 4, 92
   traffic violation, arrest without warrant . . . 21
Multi-unit premises, identification in a warrant . . . 61
Municipal ordinances
   arrest by private person . . . 31
   arrest without warrant in violation of . . . 21
   force and resistance in violation of . . . 37
   shooting or killing in violation of . . . 37

—N—

Name of accused
   affidavit as containing . . . 13
   records as containing . . . 46
   warrant as containing . . . 8, 61
No knock rule . . . 65
Notice or knowledge
   duty to submit when officer's status known . . . 39
   of intention to arrest . . . 3

of official status . . . 36
resistance, right to when officer's status not known . . . 36

—O—

Oath, necessity for in making affidavit . . . 14
Objects in plain view . . . 67, 72-73, 80, 107, 109. See also Activities in plain view
Occupation of accused, stating in warrant . . . 8
Oral consent . . . 71-72

—P—

Pardons and Paroles, State Board of, authority to issue warrants . . . 10
Parolee, warrant for . . . 10
Particularity requirements
   for affidavit . . . 63
   for search warrant . . . 60-61
Past offenses
   arrest by private person for . . . 31
   arrest without warrant for . . . 23-24
Peace officers. See officials' specific titles
   authority of (see Authority to arrest)
Peculiarities of accused, stating in warrant . . . 8
Pistol
   concealed weapon, arrest for carrying . . . 21
   shooting or killing . . . 37
Place of offense
   affidavit, stating in . . . 13, 14
   warrant, stating in . . . 7
Plain view doctrine . . . 72-73
   See also Activities in plain view and Objects in plain view
Police brutality. See Force and resistance
Posse
   authority of members . . . 32, 38-39
   citizens as . . . 38
   city police as . . . 16, 38

summoning of . . . 38-39
Possession of warrant . . . 35-36
Preliminary examination. *See* Commitment hearing
Premises, search of (Chapter 9 generally)
  curtilage . . . 60, 97-98
  description of, in warrant . . . 60-61
  forcible entry preceding . . . 65
  hotel room . . . 72, 78
  incident to arrest . . . 78-79
  landlord and tenant consent for . . . 72
  notice requirement for . . . 65
  unoccupied . . . 65
  while in hot pursuit . . . 79-80
Presence, offense committed in
  authority to make arrest for . . . 20-21
  entering private premises . . . 38
  felony, commission of . . . 20, 22
  force and resistance . . . 36-37, 39
  misdemeanor, commission of . . . 20
  municipal ordinance, violation of . . . 20
  private person, arrest by . . . 30-31
  shooting or killing . . . 37
Prison guards, jurisdiction of . . . 52
Private conversations protected . . . 104-5
Private dwelling, entering to make arrest . . . 38
Private papers, right to seize . . . 66-67
Private persons, arrest by
  bondsman . . . 32
  delay in taking accused before magistrate . . . 32-33
  duty to make arrest . . . 31
  duty upon making arrest . . . 32-33
  entering private premises . . . 38
  for felony . . . 30-31
  for misdemeanor . . . 30
  for violation of municipal ordinance . . . 31
  magistrate, duty to take prisoner before . . . 32-33

  officer making arrest outside jurisdiction, treated as private person . . . 25
  probable cause . . . 30, 31
  promptness, necessity for . . . 31
  warrant, no authority to execute . . . 30
Probable cause
  arrest with warrant . . . 10-11
  arrest without warrant . . . 23
  grand jury indictment . . . 11
  hearsay as providing . . . 11
  informant's tips supporting . . . 12-13
  private person, arrest by . . . 30-31
  reasonable grounds of suspicion . . . 11, 23, 31
Probable cause requirement
  for affidavit and issuance of search warrant . . . 62-64
  for warrantless searches . . . 74
Probation officers, jurisdiction of . . . 52
Procedure when making arrest
  assistance, summoning of . . . 38-39
  entering private premises . . . 38
  force and resistance . . . 36-37
  notice of authority . . . 36
  possession and production of warrant . . . 35-36
  shooting or killing . . . 37
  summoning of posse . . . 38-39
Production of warrant . . . 35-36
Profane language of suspect, as justifying use of force . . . 37
Property of person arrested
  care of . . . 42-43

–Q–

Questioning
  advising accused of constitutional rights before . . . 42
  of suspicious person as constituting arrest . . . 3-4

–R–

Records, duty to keep . . . 46

140 / ARREST/SEARCH AND SEIZURE

Release of accused
  for delay before commitment hearing ... 45
  for failure to notify of commitment hearing ... 44
Residence of accused, given in warrant ... 8
Resistance to arrest. *See* Force and resistance
Return of warrants
  arrest ... 17, 44
  search ... 68
Return of seized property ... 68
Revenue agents, jurisdiction of ... 51-52
Roadblocks, searches incident to ... 92-93

—S—

Safety standards, stopping automobile to check compliance with ... 4
Searches, general information. *See also* specific topics
  illegal ... Chapter 15
  with a warrant ... Chapter 9
  without a warrant ... chapters 10, 11, 12, 13
Search of person
  blood test ... 83
  breath test ... 83-84
  fingerprinting ... 84
  incident to lawful search of premises ... 65-66
  incident to lawful search of vehicle ... 97
  stop and frisk ... 81-82
  unlawful body searches ... 83
Search warrant. *See* Warrant, search
Seizure of evidence. *See* Evidence, seizure of
Self-defense
  accused, right of in resisting illegal arrest ... 36, 39
  officer, right of against accused ... 37, 75, 76, 79, 82
Sheriff
  bail, right to accept ... 45-46
  jurisdiction of ... 51

records, duty to keep ... 46
territorial extent of authority to arrest with warrant ... 16, 51
territorial extent of authority to arrest without warrant ... 25-26, 51
Shooting or killing
  in illegal arrest ... 39
  in self-defense ... 37
  to prevent escape ... 37
Silent, right of accused to remain ... 42
"Special warrants" ... 17, 44
Statutory crimes, alleging elements of ... 9
Stop and frisk ... 4, 81-82
Suspects
  automobile, stopping of ... 4
  investigation, arrest for ... 23
  investigative detention ... 3
  private person, arrest by ... 30-31
  stopping as constituting arrest ... 3
Suspicion as justifying arrest ... 23
Sworn statement. *See* Oath, necessity for in making affidavit

—T—

Telephone conversations (Chapter 14 generally)
Territorial extent of authority to arrest
  with warrant ... 16
  without warrant ... 25-27
Time
  constitutional rights, when advising person arrested ... 42
  in execution of search warrant ... 64-65
  of offense stated in affidavit ... 13, 64
  of offense stated in warrant ... 7
  of commitment hearing ... 44-45
  past offenses, arrest for ... 23-24
  promptness in arrest by private person ... 31
  promptness, necessity for in arrest without warrant ... 23-24

Traffic offenses, search incident to arrest for . . . 91-93

—U—

Uniform, authority to arrest as shown by . . . 36
Uniform Criminal Extradition Act . . . 16

—V—

Vehicle search. *See* Automobiles, search of, *and* Motor vehicles
Voluntariness of consent . . . 71-72

—W—

Waiver
  of commitment hearing . . . 44
  of constitutional rights . . . 42
Warrant, arrest
  affidavit . . . 6, 10-15
  bondsman, no requirement . . . 32
  clerk, warrant issued by . . . 10
  content requirements . . . 6-7
  county where issued, execution of outside . . . 6, 16
  designation of offense charged . . . 9
  duty to execute . . . 15
  execution of in other states . . . 16
  for extradition . . . 16
  form of . . . 8
  grand jury indictment . . . 11
  identification of person sought . . . 8-9
  informants' tips for . . . 12-13
  John Doe . . . 9
  oath, necessity for . . . 14
  officials authorized to issue . . . 9-10
  oral . . . 6
  possession and production of . . . 35-36
  probable cause, necessity for . . . 10-11
  requirements, compliance with . . . 7
  return of . . . 17, 44
  telephone . . . 6
Warrant, arrest with (Chapter 2 generally)
  authority, officer's duty to make known . . . 36
  entering private premises to execute . . . 38
  execution of warrant outside county where issued . . . 6, 16
  execution of warrant outside state where issued . . . 16
  force and resistance . . . 36-39
  identifying person sought . . . 8-9
  possession and production of warrant . . . 35-36
  private person, no authority to execute . . . 30
  who may not execute warrant . . . 15-16
  wrong person, arrest of . . . 15
Warrant, arrest without (Chapter 3 generally)
  authority, officer's duty to make known . . . 36
  by a bondsman . . . 32
  by private person . . . 30
  delay in making arrest . . . 23-24
  entering private premises to make arrest . . . 38
  felony
    arrest for . . . 20
    arrest to prevent . . . 23
  force and resistance . . . 36-37
  fugitives . . . 24
  malicious arrest . . . 11
  misdemeanor . . . 20
  municipal ordinance, for violation of . . . 20
  presence of officer, offense committed in . . . 20-21
  probable cause, necessity for . . . 23
  promptness, necessity for . . . 23-24
  territorial extent of authority . . . 25-27
  to prevent escape . . . 21-22
  to prevent failure of justice . . . 22-23

traffic violation . . . 21
when family violence has occurred
 . . . 22
Warrant, search
 contents . . . 60-61
 definition and sample copy . . . 57-59
 execution of . . . 64-68
 obtaining . . . 62

particularity requirements of . . . 60-61
 return of . . . 68
Weapons
 carrying concealed weapon . . . 21
 shooting or killing . . . 37
Wiretapping (Chapter 14 generally)
Witness, immunity of . . . 49
Wrong person, arrest of . . . 15